MEET THE EDITORS:

Tim Tim Cheng is a poet and teacher from Hong Kong, currently based between Edinburgh and London. Her pamphlet *Tapping at Glass* is out with VERVE Poetry Press in 2023. Her poems are published or anthologised in *POETRY, The Rialto, Ambit, Cicada, Our Time is a Garden,* and elsewhere. She has spoken in transnational literary panels across Asia-Pacific regions, the US, and the UK. Her latest appearances include the StAnza Poetry Festival, Hidden Door Festival, and Loop, BBC Scotland. Named 'one of the seven female poets to know in Hong Kong' by *Tatler Asia*, she is also a William Hunter Sharpe Memorial Scholarship awardee, WRiCE fellow, Roddy Lumsden Memorial Mentorship mentee, and a member of the Southbank Centre New Poets Collective.

Jason Eng Hun Lee is a poet and academic of mixed British and Malaysian Chinese ancestry whose research and practice fields encompass global anglophone literatures, postcolonial and diasporic Asian writing and global Shakespeares. His debut poetry collection *Beds in the East* was a finalist for the HKU Poetry Prize in 2010 and Melita Hume Poetry Prize in 2012. His poetry, reviews and articles have been published in *Wasafiri, Stand, Under the Radar, Acumen, Cha: An Asian Literary Journal, Quarterly Literary Review Singapore* and *Oxford Poetry*. He is a Literary Editor for *Postcolonial Text* and chief curator for OutLoud HK [隨言香港], Hong Kong's longest running poetry collective. He is a Lecturer in English and Comparative Literature at Hong Kong Baptist University.

Jennifer Wong was born and grew up in Kong Kong, is a poet, writer, researcher and translator who has published poetry, reviews and translations for many journals. Her poems have been included in books of essays and anthologies, including *Why I Write Poetry* (Nine Arches Press) and *100 Poems to Save the Planet* (Seren Books). She was a visiting fellow at Oxford TORCH for 2022 and the writer-in-residence for

Wasafiri international literature magazine in 2021. Her collection, 回家 *Letters Home*, published by Nine Arches Press in 2020, has been named a Wild Card choice by Poetry Book Society. Other works include *Goldfish* (Chameleon Press), which won the Hong Kong Arts Development Council Young Artist Award (Literary Arts), and her monograph, *Identity, Home and Writing Elsewhere in Contemporary Chinese Diaspora Poetry*, was published by Bloomsbury Academic in 2023. She has taught creative writing at Poetry School, City Lit and Oxford Brookes University.

Where Else

An International Hong Kong Poetry Anthology

Edited by Jennifer Wong, Jason Eng Hun Lee and Tim Tim Cheng

BIRMINGHAM

PUBLISHED BY VERVE POETRY PRESS
https://vervepoetrypress.com
mail@vervepoetrypress.com

FIRST PUBLISHED APR 2023
REPRINTED JULY 2023

Printed and bound in the UK
by Imprint Digital, Exeter

ISBN: 978-1-913917-36-4

Cover photo by Carmen Lau Ka Man

CONTENTS

- TWO -

- THREE -

- FIVE -

- SIX -

'Mei Wah Building' by Stella So

EDITORS' INTRODUCTIONS

1 - Jason Eng Hun Lee

The late, great, Yasi [也斯], known to fellow Anglophone poets as Leung Ping-kwan, wrote in 'Images of Hong Kong' that

> We need a fresh angle,
> nothing added, nothing taken away,
> always at the edge of things and between places.
> Write with a different colour for each voice;
> OK, but how trivial can you get?
> Could a whole history have been concocted like this?

For regular cultural observers of Hong Kong, the issue of representation has long been at the heart of much contemporary angst about the city. The challenge to provide 'a fresh angle, / nothing added, nothing taken away', to create our own individual and collective myths and resist drowning in perceptions not of our own making, has led many before us to labour to produce a more diverse, inclusive vision of what the city is and could be.

Given its history as a port of embarkation and disembarkation, Hong Kong is often said to have a diasporic mentality, spewing forth people that are comfortable inhabiting two or more cultures and locations. As Nashua Gallagher writes triumphantly, Hong Kong is 'a third-culture kid who writes her own story' ('Siu Ap Fan With a Visitor'). That ephemeral window onto the world has sometimes given Hong Kong an exotic lustre that complicates its reception as a place beyond more than just a melting pot of East and West. However, it also gives us the opportunity to reimagine what it truly means to be a community, to be more than just neighbours enclosed by borders, nationalities, identity or language.

In focusing on the ever-present nature of Hong Kong and its myriad imaginaries across the world, Jenny, Tim Tim and I humbly present to you this anthology entitled *Where Else*, which can be a statement, a question, an imperative, a declaration, or a combination of all the above. Where else but Hong Kong indeed! Yet the phrase can also be inverted to articulate that fixation on 'elsewhere', as Sam Cheuk states in 'Hoi Polloi': '"Where else / should you be?" There. Elsewhere.' If the 'real' Hong Kong is always hybrid, liminal, expressing a place in-between, an 'elsewhere' that is hard to pin down or conceptualise, it nevertheless allows us to rework these conditions into a space for meaningful exchange, where poets from all over the world can converge and take part in Leung's call to 'write with a different colour for each voice'.

While highlighting Hong Kong's connection to the wider world, the anthology celebrates the best of what can be produced or nurtured locally. Instead of producing a compendium of the 'Best of the Best' or a collection featuring the most famous, representative poets to have emerged from Hong Kong, we wanted to showcase both emerging work from our predominantly unpublished poets, whilst giving many of our veteran poets living overseas the chance to call home and reconnect with their roots. We wanted to give equal credit and weighting to all, placing grassroots voices side-by-side equally with their international counterparts and to allow the reader to dwell in their shared preoccupations.

Organised into seven sections, and with a loose thematic structure threading together the different genres and styles of our poets, we hope to produce a vibrant, contemporary vision of Hong Kong that caters to all tastes and schools. There are poems on the tangled legacies of colonialism in the city; poems on the pain of exile and the wonders of migration to and from a motherland; poems celebrating the many landmarks and geographies of Hong Kong; poems on conflict; poems on love. So too is there a veneration for the literary flag-bearers who have come before, like the aforementioned Leung Ping-kwan, Xi Xi, Louise Ho, who rightly appear as giants when mentioned by other writers in this anthology. There is also a desire to break new poetic ground, to delight in the interplay of linguistic signs and fuse together new language sensibilities as Louise Leung does in 'Brew Sky': 'Standard English meets 老一輩 when / inflexible tongues pronounce 雞腸 in 錯 geh 讀音 [...] leaving fundamental structures / with tints of Chinese saliva'. Ultimately, what the anthology hopes to achieve is to look at the city doubly from the outside as well as from the inside, to reconcile the strange with the familiar, yoke the exotic with the mundane, and to show that, despite the ever-present exotica of Hong Kong images on posters and billboards, there will always be more to say about this wonderful city and its people than can possibly be contained in a single volume.

With all our hearts, Jenny, Tim Tim and I would like to thank Stuart and his team at VERVE Poetry Press, the many poets and artists who have contributed their work, feedback and support, and the many financial (and emotional) patrons and sponsors without whom this work would not have seen the light of day. As a fellow sojourner and transnational emigre who can claim multiple heritages, Hong Kong has never felt more like home. Yet home is, as many of the poems have shown, as much an imaginative concept as a physical one. If the anthology opens with a sense of one's memories trapped in the past, it ends with the realisation, in Hilary Tam's poem, that 'home' will never leave us. It is with this in mind that we dedicate this anthology to our wider Hong Kong family stretched out across the oceans, but also to those who write in conditions that do not always make art-making easy, to the various groups and collectives that labour week-in, week-out, to put up a space for writers of all stripes and colours to read, listen, or share their work and to break bread with their fellow poets in communion, and to help nurture and publish the next generation. This book is for you all.

2 - Jennifer Wong

In co-editing this anthology with Jason and Tim Tim, I was reminded of the days when I started out as a poet writing in and from Hong Kong. My friends used to tease me: *you want to write about Hong Kong? What's there to write about, pollution?* Now, in 2023, as we launch this anthology, I can't help but feel proud about this book because if I were a young writer coming from Hong Kong, I would love to read it. It's an anthology that can give a Hong Kong writer the courage and permission to write from the heart (even if English is not one's mother tongue). This book is affirming in the sense that I know I'm not alone.

In the process of our editing and soliciting submissions from the open call, I am exhilarated to discover the sheer range of voices emerging from this place, some of whom I have not encountered before. Best of all, I fall in love with poems that offer bold and refreshing ways to read Hong Kong, such as 'Demi-Noblesse' where we see a customer's quiet moment in a local cha chaan teng (Hong Kong-style cafe), her orders 'clipped and exact', who hopes to lead a life that is 'a little elegant, a little kind / even as my city falls apart'. From MTR train rides (such as in Kika Man's '請勿靠近車門' and Michael Tsang's 'Reading Louise Ho on the MTR'), mahjong games ('||: 碰 :||' by Josephine Yip), pandemic abnormalities (Polly Ho's 'Leaving at Night'); a lunar calendar (Sarah Howe's 'Calendar') to the natural landscape in Hong Kong (e.g. Kate Rogers's 'The Young Biologists'), these poems revel in the power of poetry to transform the everyday into something extraordinary.

In our compilation process, we were impressed to see the poets' courage and originality in addressing conflicts, whether they are class barriers, inequality, struggles with racial, gender, queer identities or relationships, challenges living under strict Covid restrictions, and surviving the city's ineradicable memories and traumatic changes. In 'Madame X' by Jessica Chan and 'The Last Words of a Dying Girl' by Swann Adara Lee, for example, it is impossible not to be moved by the speaker's longing for social acceptance, for an end to unfair biases against queer love.

As a school student in Hong Kong, I remember reading poems by Louise Ho and Agnes Lam, and loving the way they brought the city to life through writing about the multicultural, the local rituals or working class spaces. I have also been encouraged by how they claimed their subjectivities as Asian woman writers. Later, reading Agnes Lam's research *Becoming Poets**—in which she traces the writing practice, cultural and linguistic backgrounds of generations of Asian poets including poets from Hong Kong—has brought new understanding and hopes that Hong Kong poetry must be heard and to claim its unparalleled space in world literature. As scholars, critics and poets, Jason Lee and Tammy Ho have interviewed Asian diasporic poets in Singapore and Hong Kong to capture the Anglophone city poetics and Asian experience, pose new questions on the multiplicities of Asian writing and the cultural identity of these writers.

Having relocated from Hong Kong to live in England a decade ago, I realised that my writing community and landscape do not fall neatly in a single place, even though I have always seen myself as a writer from Hong Kong. At the same time, I am fortunate enough to be connected with a diverse diasporic writing community, including some very talented Hong Kong poets in the UK and the US. In his prize-winning essay 'The "Old Hong Kong" and "a Gold-sifting Bird": Hong Kong and Chinese Ekphrasis in Contemporary British Poetry' published in *Wasafiri*, poet-critic Antony Huen expands on the concept of 'Hong Kong poetry', its ekphrastic roots as well as geopolitical nature that encompasses 'cultural memory, and diaspora, and the complex geopolitical relations between Hong Kong, mainland China, and the UK'.

To me, it seems that there isn't a clear-cut, stable definition of what a 'Hong Kong poet' is. What we would like to bring about is the space and willingness for people to appreciate these writings, and I can't wait to see how readers will respond to the thematic and geographical range of voices that we have captured, and to discover the dialogues between their works.

I am indebted to fellow poets and co-editors Jason and Tim Tim, for their insights, dedication and friendship in the process, and I am deeply touched by their willingness to embrace all kinds of poets or poems that deserve to be in the book. We are tremendously grateful to those who have supported us throughout the creative process, especially Stuart Bartholomew at VERVE, who has believed in the project since the beginning. Thanks to our patrons and friends who care about this anthology, and readers—you who are reading this right now—and we hope that you will enjoy discovering such a diverse range of original and essential voices from Hong Kong.

---

* Agnes Lam, *Becoming Poets* (Bern: Peter Lang, 2014)

3 - Tim Tim Cheng

It was a humbling experience editing *Where Else: An International Hong Kong Poetry Anthology*. I came across so many well-written poems that I wish I had written myself. Reading more than 400 entries—some by poets I admire, some by poets I have never met—I am both moved and proud of being able to contribute to one of Hong Kong's many writing communities. The book you are holding is a labour of love, in which poets who are faithful to their crafts come together to acknowledge their connections with this small dot of a place we call Hong Kong.

Without reading Hong Kong poets, I would not know our stories deserved a place in English verse. Our curricula have always been farsighted. We learn to care about what is far away in time and space more than the here and now. I am grateful for Hong Kong anthologies published by *Cha: An Asian Literary Journal*, *Voice & Verse Poetry Magazine* and VERVE Poetry Press, Cart Noodle Press, Chameleon Press, OutLoud HK, and *Canto Cutie*, among others, for showing an aspiring poet like me what is possible in the making of Hong Kong literature. We are not the first who do this, and we will surely not be the last.

It is good to know that you are not alone, and things you care about share common values with people beyond your wildest imagination. This, to me, is the purpose of our anthology. I want readers who identify as Hongkongers to feel understood and empowered. I want readers who are not familiar with Hong Kong to be surprised by the city's multitudes. I want readers who are somewhere between the two groups to keep being curious about the city. I do wonder, though, if our anthology will be valuable not just among academics and writers. I am speaking as a secondary school teacher who believes that words are vessels of power. Being attentive to them could make a difference in the ways we relate ourselves to the world.

In Wong Yi's interview with Dung Kai-cheung titled 'The Hong Kong Type', Dung contends that: '[t]here is no such thing as 'Hong Kong history'—everyone has their own Hong Kong history. I think it's more important for everyone to have their own history of Hong Kong than one official, unified history of Hong Kong.' Our stories are proliferating and gaining more attention in times of crisis. It is both bottom-up and top-down. This anthology attempts to gather diverse representations while ensuring that honesty, safety, and marketability are in balance. The suffix '-ty' seems to reflect that one has to think of Hong Kong as a state that complicates, and a condition that requires care.

When Jennifer, Jason, and I selected poems we were entrusted with, it was a learning process for all of us, too. There were moments in which we Googled street names because we had never heard of them. They sounded 'too foreign' to be 'the Hong Kong in our minds'. There were moments in which we could not locate the description in a poem, only to be told by the poet that it was an important historical site. As much as the three of us have been Hong Kong residents at different points of our lives, it is crucial that we do not conflate our biographies with ethnic and/or cultural credibility as we set out to consolidate a certain 'Hong Kong poetics'.

Hong Kong writing is a slippery thing, not to mention the space that Anglophone Hong Kong poets occupy. As Dorothy Tse Hiu Hung summarises: 'are we writing in a mother tongue when we write in Chinese? [...] It is a written vernacular based mainly on Mandarin. [...] To us, this written Chinese is neither Mandarin nor Cantonese. [...] So when we start to write, we are already being detached from our daily life; we are already somebody else.' Most Hongkongers' daily life escapes linguistic essentialism. Some of our featured poets bridge the gap between living and writing by code-switching and/or amplifying accents in their work. Their refusal to translate meanings into (loose) English equivalents stretch what a good Anglophone poem could be.

During the course of editing our anthology, I went to the launch of several anthologies, such as *More Fiya: A New Collection of Black British Poetry* (edited by Kayo Chingonyi) and *Converse: Contemporary Indian Poetry in English* (edited by Sudeep Sen). Poets as post-colonial subjects are constantly negotiating what is lost and found in the imaginative act of translating (lived) experiences onto the page. What does it mean to write from / towards / around / beyond one's position(s)? Asserting one's heritage in one's work is a double-edged sword. It is reductive, if not harmful, to insist that every poem coming from a historically marginalised group must be urgent, autobiographical, or contain identifiable markers.

I recall a Kei Miller essay titled 'In Defense of Maas Joe'. The problem of an overused trope is less about the trope itself but the fact that the writing fails to convince. I will leave the reader to decide if the Hong Kong tropes assembled in our anthology qualify as something insightful and exciting. In the same essay, Miller stresses that: 'to build a house is to simultaneously create two locations – an outside and an inside, and so when we create a house for our national literatures we should immediately be conscious of and interrogate not only who we include, but who we exclude'.

Try as we might, our anthology is not exhaustive. I hope we could serve as a springboard for more anthologies, more voices to come.

Where Else

An International Hong Kong Poetry Anthology

'A Humid Day' by Wahyan Au

ONE

‘A tyre-skirted ferry edges towards
dock caught in its endless crossing,
back and forth, forth and back’

(‘Calendar’, Sarah Howe)

Sestina for Hong Kong

May Huang

Before I return to the disappearing city
For weeks I have the same dream
Of a maze built on reclaimed land, an old house,
A locked door down the hallway of memory
'You'll be back home before too long,'
They say, back to the sound of falling rain

Back home, I can count on the rain
To cascade over the invisible city
Here, patience is short and traffic jams long
And boats on the harbor whistle a pipe dream
Here, stop by the cha chaan ting for a plate of memory:
Char siu rice, two eggs, and milk tea on the house

Mold fell like fresh snow over our house
Thanks to the unrelenting August rain
Washing the skyscrapers, washing away memory
I guess it's time to say farewell to the city
I throw out old schoolwork, rusted glasses, a dream
Catcher. Mother says selling the house won't take long

Still, Neruda said "forgetting is so long"
I remember dressing up and playing house
Back when there was little to do but dream
Practicing my name meant writing out rain
Eight strokes, every line mapping out the city
Until characters fade like photos from my memory

When butterfly lovers fly into *Speak, Memory*
Those carefree days will have been long
Gone. In California I reread Xixi's *My City*
By the magnolia trees, in a stranger's house
I'm near the ocean again but there's hardly any rain
Only the bitter myth of the American dream

Whatever happened to the Hong Kong dream?
Landmarks vanish from our collective memory
Bauhinias wilt in the unforgiving rain
Tai O, Hang Hau, and Yuen Long
The places I wrote poems about after we moved house
The summer grief taught me to love the city

One summer I'll dream of a maze again and long
For childhood, now just a memory of years spent in that house
Listening to rain, learning to leave the city

Eye

Claire Cox

Always a girl's name –
you knew she was near
by the clamp of your dress
on the skin between

your shoulder blades.
And the thunder ants
that thudded against the lamp's
hot silk to mill

across the parquet floor,
dropping their wings
in brittle scatterings.
You'd pick one up,

place its wonderment
in your palm and run
to show your parents. The air
would stir. Out over

the balcony, the harbour
and the triangled lights of ships,
the night clotting,
a thickness on your tongue,

there must have been lighting,
gusts that rattled the neon signs
down in Wan Chai, rain
like ticker-tape –

but what you remember
is the lull, and your father
calling you to the balcony,
circling you in his arms

to watch a porthole of stars
pass overhead, its vast disc
shared like a held breath.

Build and Dismantle

Emerald Liu

Between the concrete and bamboo
the sky and sea melt
views shift
and scrape my retina
trying to remember the composition of each street
but with each return I see the city changing
I try to pinpoint landmarks
the way my father does
to orientate
the city hall, their honeymoon hotel, his college bookstore
between the new walkways and offices
marrying the old with the new
the sentiment with the practical
this city is a maze
I will mold it in my memory
build on memories which I make my own
this city is a maze
in which I centre myself

Calendar
Sarah Howe

Unearthed in a clear-out, a picture calendar she's kept
hoarding, I've learnt, is a mark of the emigrant

across continents and time. *Beautiful Hong Kong 1983*
reads the cover's winking skyline, not quite idiomatically.

The comb-bound pages, flipsides mottled, stick
each month a panoramic vista shot from up the Peak

or other island spots, full-colour photography
faded now as silk wallpaper Chinoiserie.

How quaint it seems, my birth-year, or how colonial:
Birthday of Her Majesty sits days from *Tuen Ng Festival.*

In January's foreground, an orange-tiled pagoda
pops from scrubby mountainside above the skyscrapers,

their bar-chart ranks washed-out against the harbour's blue,
where a haze of rain turns down the contrast on Kowloon.

A sense that something's off, then suddenly it dawns
the tallest of the needles pinned through the coast are gone

or rather not-yet-there; the time-travel uncanny
like spotting the twin towers intact in an 80s movie.

I picture it: the waterfront a juddering time-lapse
where buildings fall and rise like the Hang Seng index

cocooned in a greenish shroud of scaffolded bamboo
to emerge at cloud-level, gleaming and improbable

the sky's bright hem-line creeping ever higher
while junks skim like fiery leaves across a pond's mirror.

Count back nine fingers: February. The month that I sparked
into being, a whorl of cells. In the print, fireworks

like red anemones cast their glow over starlit water,
office blocks ghostly from the long exposure.

March: the green Peak tram chugs up a jungled incline.
I have eyelids now (still fused), a crescent moon of spine.

I flip ahead to June, which frames the exact aspect
from the windows of our family's long-gone flat:

once you've left, home turns into something foreign.
My kicks are butterflies, my length a handspan.

August: dusk, and the city's purpled high-rises
disappear beneath a glaze of sky in famille-rose

only to reinvent themselves in blinking neon,
as traffic streaks the streets with white-hot ribbons.

By the last trimester, each puffing step's a strain.
The truth is, you can't ever quite come home again.

On October's spread, an orphaned clocktower
in reddish brick, marooned on a demolished shore.

Note how the 14th has been highlighted in yellow:
she did mention that I was two weeks overdue.

December: a tyre-skirted ferry edges towards dock
caught in its endless crossing, back and forth, forth and back.

Citizen Ship

David McKirdy

For Leung Ping Kwan

We arrived on the same day
you in the hold of a fishing junk
me on the ocean liner.
Settling into a three-story house
the shipping crates were delivered by noon
discarded, they made a hut for you on the hill.

We lived on either side of the same street
kept apart by the wall between
a physical and symbolic shield
to prevent disease, or 'going native'.

We tried to connect
but concrete and closed minds are tough to conquer
a barrier for inhibitions carelessly thrown
not so for hurled rocks and insults.

We flew kites across the top
swooping and dancing as one
the caress
then the cut of the string.

We learned each other's tongue
through jagged gaps
"Good morning" - "Jo san"
"How are you?" - "Nei ho ma?"
"What is your name?" - "Nei gieu mut yeh meng?"
"Well fuck your mother!" - "Dieu nei lo mo!"

We left home together for school
you on foot
me on the bus
attending classes at either end of another street
both burdened by the hopes and expectations
of another generation.

We arrived on the same day
grew up together - apart.
One colony - two systems
two people - one future.

Two Candles (婉)

Robert Black

'We came through cold daylight to get here,
following a trail of broken glass.'— Ping Kwan Leung

蠟燭

The wind takes its voice from the shape of his spindly body in the rain
as it syllables itself gulping at air
wrapped in vowels and promises the shape of stride and settling
and it enters
but he is turning and it is blue-late and the world is astride in eventide.
From that, an infant hiss tickles itself through the space between the curve of the yard
and the tooth-gap in the window's screening:
gas or flag-linen wrapping some incandescent exhalation,
slow burn tugging against an expiration.
He turns and turns some more until now a final pitch
and he awakes swaying.

How quickly the middle of the river's night candles this awakening,
that running for which he has sought comfort
when stranded and webbed and shuttlecocked
past the counting of sleep's arithmetic and the stumbling blocks of the world:
he listens and wades out into the darkness as it bobbins him,
past the over-burdened book shelves and warped belly of the front door,
along the mongoose's path and alleys into a lane--
he is incandescent with sound,
stands biding for sight and unfolds.
She is twelve time zones away.

Bent toward the hanging plants all-around,
the eaves and easements and evening song, allieved,
his body necks shapely as it adjusts itself from sleep
images patter through him much quicker than the acuity of his eyes,
once there was the spout from the cast iron kettle they both sucked upon,
varicose with thumb print and lifeline,
the dried-leaf stains on his Uniqlo sleeves, the map she drew with her toes in his bedding,
the Tai Chi of the vertical and horizontal, and their bridging and collapsing of language,
their night walking now his armature as he waits,
her smile unfolded once as Chrysanthemum in warm water,
the toys toppled from a table box,
and he gathers all of that and breathes and the world is spinning.
An ocean away, she awakes.

As the hours clack and rattle, the muscular silence softens,
he listens once again to the indiscriminate chirping
and recognizes the bruised night, voices of children lit up
in the trees and tangled in joy, their reckoning from branch to branch,
catscradle stories as they scampered from limb to limb,
younger children steadfast in their street sleep at that hour.
He speaks to her of this once and sends his words aloft, a candle weaving the dark.

Time later, he lotus on the floor begins to count names he will not write,
Memorize the scars he will not suture, the sweat he will not cloth
and the words he will not swallow--
he tucks the touch of loss in a pocket,
the gravitational pull of the names he will not say directly, the words he will not pen,
the tug real as falling clatter a balcony away.
And while basketing all he ventures to say there again is that small hiss
and a small burning of heat which he sees but cannot take in with skin.

Across the road there it is, the origin of the sound:
Là zhú.
a small candle winking in a window:
the name and thing that had awoken him
a flagging gently in a neighbor's window.
It speaks to him of her though she is 10,000 li away:
婉.

One syllable soft to the touch and rounded as silk, cocoon of language,
character which pens beautiful and filled by grace
her name and words which once built him a room with when she spoke:
each candle in a window,
each child in a tree,
each clip of him that runs
toward the distance, unending,
the uptake and the coupled upbraiding of each.
蠟燭, 喜喜, bejewelled and unbending.

He can not forget and pockets his eyes and his body spills
Swoon of gravity pulling gently at his side and the light marks him with scent
and he pivots sleep and a rich unsteadying:
婉婉 and the wand from which the wax butters
alights music and wintering,
sets aglow fright or the abacus of loss
green palms ringing the bones and verbs of your own flight.

The narrative or the interpretation,
the sway of body or its syntax,
a lexicon of failure or of hope?
Who can, even once, imagine?

One day a clocking in the city's body at the end of time.

Yung Shue Wan Pier

Helen Bowell

We're walking the gangplank again, bumping our suitcases over its yellow hyphens, the tang of aeroplane on the ceilings of our mouths. The workers are shouting, pulling the boat to, arms like rope. The air is filled with trolleys trundling and relatives *hi!*-ing family home, *wah*, how they've grown, look what they've brought to eat. Now we're late for dinner with your sister, for a meal that will bridge the two years between you. Now it's morning and we're rushing to catch the 10.30. There is dim sum ahead, hours of tea and clean shopping centres. We sit by the opened windows, ask for the breeze and the engine's oily breath. Now we're waking our legs from the ferry, for the dark walk into the hills and home. Our beds this time are in your mother's flat. Now they're in your childhood home. Now the farm's ex-pigsty, air conditioned and new. Now we're hurrying back to the ferry in wedding clothes we're trying not to sweat-mark. Your nephew's getting married, now your niece. The air feels like warm seawater. We drink it breathlessly like tea. Now we're early for the next boat because we missed the one before. We're never early on purpose. We're pulling Vitasoys from the vending machine and they taste like all our pink stationery. We're taking a deep look with our lungs, listening to the fishermen's whip-cast, their deckchairs shufling on the pier, their sips of Lipton Iced Tea. This is the photo I'm trying to take: here, by the bicycles, peering over the edge.

New Territories

Sean Wai Keung

Mr H watches his reflection in the tolo harbour
ripple as the tide slowly pushes against the pier he sits on
Mr H thinks about his grandfather
who worked the boats here decades ago
Mr H worries about his own grandchildren
living on the other side of the world now
Mr H wonders how different the sea might be
in a place like brighton in england
Mr H considers again how much it would cost
if he was to fly over there to visit grandson
Mr H counts through time zones and realises
that grandson should be going for his morning sea swim right now
Mr H looks up and his eyes meet the flashing lights
of a building standing tall in the distance
Mr H chastises himself briefly
for not being rich enough to own a private boat or jet
Mr H pictures his grandfather again
his hunched over back and face wrinkled by years of smoking
Mr H realises that if grandson is swimming in the sea right now
if he touches the sea here then all there will be is sea between them both
Mr H tentatively reaches a hand out towards the water below him
imagining grandson front crawling through choppy waves
Mr H has to stretch further down to reach it
and eventually his fingertips drop through the surface
Mr H is surprised by how cold the water is
although he supposes it must be colder in brighton in england
Mr H suddenly flickers through time briefly
the reflection of his face for a second taking on the form of another

Mr H closes his eyes and lets out a long and deep sigh
while in brighton in england the tide slowly comes in
Mr H focuses all his energy on transmitting one final message
why dont you call me more he emits

and then im so proud of you

With Wings You Gave Me

Nadee

For my Grandmother

You shaped and coloured the wings
I used to fly
when I was small
when I had to learn things

More familiar to me than my mother
You kept me in your arms
even if there was no milk in your breast
the love you gave was as pure as the white flower

You bathed and saved me like a lotus in a lake
and when I finally stood on my own
you and my mother laughed joyfully that day

When I cannot sleep
I do not know the
constellation
I think of how you are closest to me
like a shelter for my heart
When I think of you, Grandmother,
I feel the center of my heart

So far so good
You are never far...
when I see the first star shining in the night sky
You're the one I see.

How Did I Forget?

Ethan Yu

How did I forget
how cold a winter
in Sacramento
can be?

How did I forget
how long it's been
since I've returned
back home?

I don't remember
my mother in spring
planting the four cypress trees
in our front yard.

I don't remember
my mother bringing
me and my brother to press our hands
on the cold and wet concrete.

I don't know
where they are now.
At the feet of the cypress trees,
my mother's roses have grown.

Repulse Bay Hotel, Hong Kong (1981)

Harry Ricketts

Soon, they say, this elegant façade
will exist only in photos; for some,

a shard of post-imperial tristesse;
for others, more colonial scar-tissue.

But here this morning on the quiet verandah,
breakfast in ruins around you, looking

out through ropes of rain, falling
on the steps, the beach, the empty bay,

you find yourself shuddering suddenly
to think of all those, gwai-lo and Chinese,

who have sat, like you, watching
distant flame-trees scarlet out of green.

Bauhinia x Blakeana

Antony Huen

Her chow mein tasted like home and
we slurped it. Some bean sprouts drooped
from your lip and you looked like the flower
of my city. I call it 洋紫荊 (yeung-zhi-ging),
meaning foreign purple thorns. She'd say
yang-zi-jing but drop the *yang*.

In the attic, we learnt from Google
that it's sterile, hermaphroditic,
named after Sir Henry
and Lady Blake. On Street View,
we spotted through its blossoms
my bedroom back home.

Our eyes travelled to York
Castle on a hill of daffodils.
Two boys sat on the slopes, basking
in the yang of the English sun.
Their faces blurred, no access to
what's behind the private sign.

Siu Ap Fan with a Visitor

Nashua Gallagher

"What was it like to grow up in Hong Kong?"
"Do you speak Cantonese?"
Sometimes, it was like living in the waiting room of an airport.
And like in the airport, everything is translated three times,
So no, I don't speak Cantonese.

I tell her, I am my own brand of local;
The kind that doesn't carry an umbrella with me.
Come 6 o'clock my contact lenses feel like peanut brittle.
I too, am an MTR test-tube baby; earphones umbilical to device that lets me recline fetal in my mind.
I have the right to land and an accent that won't settle.

We are in line for Siu Ap Fan,
Realizing too late, this was not a meal for two.
All that bone spitting and rice shoveling,
It's for sinewy fragments-in-your-teeth kind of thinking.
Fat sizzles on crispy duck skin and runs down your chin,
We slurp and gnaw and revel, all teeth and no conversation.

The duck man's lunch grind requires a strut that is;
Part mother hen, part factory supervisor,
A furrowed brow, cleaver
Heave-ho'ing,
Clang-bang people traffic, an instant spill into the streets like
a fresh teabag in water. Bo le slammed down next to me, chopsticks
rattle, and a plus on my ticket tells them to call order six
Not lok.
My duck man knows how to cater to those like me.
She asks about sovereignty.

I talk about the trees on Hollywood road, branches procumbent,
Snaking like varicose veins on the island's asphalt skin,
Money pumped into mountains scraped back,
Only to have its soil entailed to northern cousins.
Sometimes it takes a little ingenuity,
To build bricks out of a make believe place,
Like a plus on a ticket,
A white bauhinia amongst the red,
Because you see, Hong Kong, like me
is a third culture kid who writes her own story.

Island

Louise Ho

We are a floating island
Kept afloat by our own energy
We cross date lines
National lines
Class lines
Horizons far and near

We are a floating island
We have no site
Nowhere to land
No domicile

Come July this year
We may begin to hover in situ
May begin to settle
May begin to touch down
We shall be
A city with a country
An international city becoming national

英年早逝

Felix Chow Yue Ching

The newspaper copies are copies. A scrapbook of self.
All show the same glittering face of the harbour
named Victoria: a foreign monarch whose
(as of recent) rule we were never under.

We learn 事頭婆 stirred shit, 肥彭 was fibbing,
white hands cleaved city from nation.
A raising of flags. A change of curriculum.
The ground which we stood on torn open.

We're asked to churn
our own ocean-pored bones.
Let them lie, lie, more closely
Take what is left, carefully sift it through safenets.
Scrub youthful faces from memory.

Leave grey flower-pots where white words
baked by sun, used to lie. Ulcer our minds.
Shed the screams from our spines
in dark night, witnessed by floodlights.

Like our great-grandmothers,
who ate dead bark from trees
We fabricate new plastic flowers.
Plant them in concrete heaped over sand
grey hands reclaiming what's ours.

'The Occupiers' by Wahyan Au

TWO

'the singing of our bodies to keep
the land alive'

('exodus hong kong', Xiao Yue Shan)

The Dotted Line

Mani Rao

How many oceans is a question
in schools.

Four, five, or one, depending
on your vintage and philosophy.

We know Canadian gulls deported
in the spray of Niagara, held in U.S. custody.

Of Hong Kong dogs that crossed the line,
and vanished in mainland eateries.

Said a whale to its calf, don't go too far,
Watch where you jump.

I'm a little concerned, the southern ocean
is now called the Southern Ocean.

If You Don't Hit It, It Won't Fall

Sarah Howe

Young we were, schoolmates, at life's
full flowering. Do not say

the waters of Kunming Lake
are too shallow, rolling back

the enemy like a mat.
My mother asked, Why are you

so upset? I told her I
fancied a pair of skating

shoes. The ants on the locust
tree assume a great-nation

swagger. Away with all pests!
Sparrow replies, Look, the world

is being turned upside down.
A pair of skating shoes will

shore up the falling heaven.
O, I want to flit away

to a jewelled palace: beef-filled
goulash, potatoes piping

hot. There'll be plenty to eat.
I've searched every street and still

can't find them. The world rolls on.
Time presses. I felt a force

moving my feet. People here
call it the city of lights –

the universe is glowing
red. Where are we bound? Some things

I've already forgotten.
I remember how gunfire

licks at the heavens, awesome
for dancing. Stop your windy

nonsense! Even now the red
flag of revolution swells

with the skateboard shoes I want.
Wild bears never daunt the brave.

She said one day I will find
them. She said only heroes

can quell tigers and leopards.
She said time will tell. Just as

I was about to give up
I saw a specialty store:

nothing is hard in this world
if you dare to scale the heights.

Plum blossom welcomes my new
skate shoes, so fashionable

under the bright autumn moon.
I tell myself this is not

a dream. Six hundred million
people rub it on this smooth

dancefloor. With my skateboard shoes
I'm not afraid of the night.

Note: This poem is stitched together from language found in two sources: *Poems* by Mao Zedong (trans. Open Source Socialist Publishing, 2008) and the Chinese viral pop sensation 'My Skating Shoes' by Pang Mailang (trans. ChinaSmack, 2014).

Special Economic Zone Love Song

Jane Wong

These days, I'm floundering.
The skin of the ocean crisps

at daybreak. There is too much
vegetation in my ears.

Broccoli limbers up in the grooves,
sprouting vertigo.

*

The signs of a bottle factory
shine in laminate.

Fog kisses each and every cheek.
On a LCD screen, the sun rises

in pixelated elation, sweeping
the bangs from our eyes.

A snail in basil takes
its daily jaunt along

oil slicks. Pork hangs
from a balcony,

salting. A button unfastens
under a bright light.

It's hard, this desire
for company in bitter

weather. Mid-day, a worker
plants bitter greens

under a highway.
There is this flavor

of char in every vein,
worth every penny

in every century.

*

To be a stranger, I held
onto my best disguise.

When you reach for me
like this, fleas bite

through my socks
as we kiss and kiss.

*

Everyone falls into a river
at least once.

Not everyone gets saved.
I've been loitering

among heroes again.
Construction workers lunch

in the open field. Smoke
unwraps in lettuce.

A cow drenched in rain
stands uncontrollably.

To enter the factory,
you have to announce yourself

by punching in, not by
throwing a punch.

I can get so hysterical
sometimes, so lightheaded.

Sometimes the run-off
colors the water where the cranes

dip their necks as they listen
to the waltz

of a wrecking ball.

Border Town

Viki Holmes

The people on the other side of the invisible line
are just the same, the uniforms vary in colour
but the guards stand as straight, lean back
to avoid cameras with the same easy care.

She stands on a balcony built for five
belonging to the restaurant
with Sunday morning's chickens' feet
and chopsticks heaped on circular tablecloths.
The same flowers grow, the same birds cross
the invisible line with the same
insouciance
whichever side they came from.

Her side has a tree fat with oranges, bigger
than her head; the last Queen's postbox
in Hong Kong, the village representative
paints for them the colours underneath,
the gilt and scarlet of the crown. But
they are all village representatives here,
he says. And she looks on at the woman

crossing the invisible line, feather duster
in hand. Going to clean the same dust
that settles here. And thinks of home
she will not call, or touch, or dream,
but will return, to her own side,

as though nothing at all had changed.

exodus hong kong

Xiao Yue Shan

1

listen carefully—there is land or there is water,
and a time where
you may mistake one for another.
there is day and there is night,
the only difference between them
is that a body may pass through one living
to arrive at the other no longer.

2

if by land, you will travel
through the wutong mountains. follow the path
to liantang, cross over in luofang.
bring as much food as you can. remember your name
and where you are going. you will have to say the words
like you are not starving.

3

at the red marks of painted
stone, by the mangroves there,
I watched once a child searching
the pockets of his father
who laid perfectly still in the summer stones,
mouth filling with the rising river.

4

water is through the throat of baishizhou, across
shenzhen bay. there will be men scanning the paths,
so send your body low and fast
into the long taste of salt. the sea—
it is hong kong's. they will not take
you back from it. it is the first test of the other side's
forgiveness, to enter admitting you belong nowhere,
that you are no one.

5

dandelion, banana skins, the stems of sweet potatoes. to boil
the roots of a mountain fern for its starch. to stew grass until
a dark vegetal paste collects in the pot, and the tongue thickens
with mosses and oils. bright scream of hunger ripping the body
into constellations. famine has a smell—
sunned ashes grey-yellow in the shapeless
winter silence.

6

those that fed on barks and grasses would swell—
flesh holding impressions like clay. how seldom we think
about the substance of our bodies, unnoticed until
it must be endured, red seared skin heavy in liquid
bloom. it was better when
the people you loved stopped looking
like themselves. like watching a stranger die.

7

all this has been made by mothers into song.

8

we were arriving by the hundreds and so did not look
like people any longer. the elderly, the young, men, women, camphors,
wires, rain—all questions. it was the sea
that swam through me. someone calls my name
as if they were ripping it from my body.

9

forty years later on the shenzhen side a man
carves a passage in the lobby
of a luxury hotel and travels back
forty years through it. *he was carrying me*
on his back before he fell. his hand
accusing the earth strangling
the bullet air.

10

what we knew of the new world?
barbed fence twenty kilometres long, earth-burn,
salt-lick. prying my mother's hands
hardened around a willow branch. white-eyed watchdogs
carving their lethal arc in the spine. one tests
the fit of death upon him, putting it on like fire
puts on smoke. we ran
taking what we knew with us.

11

the singing of our bodies to keep the land alive.
the singing of our bodies to keep the land alive.

How We Survived: 爺爺's Pantoum (II)

River 瑩瑩 Dandelion

we wore watermelon husks to hide
lost cargo floating east to hong kong
water lilies & crickets our last witness
we departed the cattailed creek one final time.

lost cargo floating east to hong kong
new hing dai treaded water, compasses toward freedom
we departed the cattailed creek one final time
white sharks awaited our legs in the depths.

new hing dai treaded water, compasses toward freedom
they said we had an 80% chance of making it
white sharks awaited our legs in the depths
$\frac{\text{breath + breath × wanting}}{\text{death}} =$

an 80% chance of making it
letters sent back announced survival.
$\frac{\text{breath + breath × wanting}}{\text{death}}$
banked on generations of dreaming

letters sent back announced survival.
we were promised work in the restaurants
banked on generations of dreaming
fishermen took pity & reeled us on gasoline tanks.

we were promised work in the restaurants
i clawed brown earth before collapsing.
fishermen took pity & reeled us on gasoline tanks
five bowls of rice in hong kong, my sweetest meal.

i clawed brown earth before collapsing
villagers found us gasping, fish out of water
five bowls of rice in hong kong, my sweetest meal.
memories escape me now.

villagers found us gasping, fish out of water.
my thoughts enter one ear & leave the other.
memories escape me now.
you being here helps me remember.

my thoughts enter one ear & leave the other.
water lilies & crickets, our last witness.
you being here helps me remember
we wore watermelon husks to hide.

for 爺爺
in memoriam

爺爺 — yeh yeh, Cantonese for paternal grandfather
hing dai — Cantonese for brothers or close friends

(a)bridge(d)

Sophie Lau

worth more than daughters
pigs are saved first in fire and flood
quick! over the threshold
our golden house rule
remember your place

little girls lug rice across the border
destined for mothers
in paddy fields
sing a red song
pay respect to the chairman
not all respect needs to be earned but
all keep does

beneath a bridge a baby cries
mother   in law
saviour   executioner
taught never to cry when faced with hard labour
she bears six children for her brother

one generation away
red digits rise up
her daughter catches the taxi driver's eye
driven from new territories to old
small island to great
white surrender lies
in both flags

「妹豬」

je me suis rendu
compte que l'amour pour nous
tout
faux
destin en vue
place déjà connue
golden rule defined by you

sing

「東方紅
太陽升」

respect

毛澤東。
明不明？

婆婆不明？
這些話

cows are sold
driven from their homes
too fragile to shoulder rice
daughters are yoked
worth their weight in gold
pigs are nourished for a destiny
of slaughter

habla historia
[insert hakka]
por ahora
dura vida
redactada

「妹豬，97到了」

cycle rompu
we start anew

Self-portrait of My Granny in the Voice of Anti-Japanese Drama's Protagonists

Tim Tim Cheng

I, full of passion and education,
was trained in martial arts. I could jump high—
up to the sixth floor. I loved my nation
despite having five passports. You asked why
I couldn't handle my grandchild's homework
and never moved to another country.
The point is, the Japanese are the worst.
It's true, the show, our soldiers fought bravely.
With bare hands, we could halve our enemy.
Yes, I was sent to farms during uni.
Yes, dad gave up his land to dodge assaults
but Mao Zhuxi's deeds did outweigh his faults.
          I miss you. I'm glad you're back to see me.
          Do you want some of these salmon sushi?

My Mother's Love

Tegan Smyth

My mother's love is
yelling at me to dry my hair after a shower,
lest I get sick.
My mother's love is
force-feeding 青木瓜鱼汤 when I was a teen,
eyeballing every last morsel left in a bowl.
My mother's love is
never providing a direct compliment and
hearing words of warmth second hand.
My mother's love is
bleaching every square inch
of the house when the occupants are outside.
My mother's love is
washing and cutting fruit
on the same board that smells like onions.
My mother's love is
advice like powdered Chinese medicine,
taken hot and bitter but giving clarity where needed.
My mother's love is
buying a snack I said I liked once
for the next ten years.
My mother's love is
when she complains about my crochet
but wears the clothes I make for her.
My mother's love is
overhearing her yell at strangers who say my Canto sucks
by saying "my daughter speaks 4 languages - what about you?"
My mother's love is
the walks we go on sometimes
with no destination in mind.

Ping Shan Heritage Trail

Akin Jeje

Only an act of pragmatism
keeps this journey
of pre-Hong Kong
alive.

Ten frayed monuments
In solemn successions,
like those
parchment-faced grandmas
tottering gradually through
e-impatient crowds.

Little feeling
from the bustle; ignoring what's past
few here
treasure relics without a price.
Temples graying, village walls thick with moss,
dusted curios,
rusted paths,
final memoriam of a forgotten age.

Kids pass noisily
eyes intent on hand-held Game Boys™
I the foreign, the only face
searching in vain, through newness
for secrets in stone skulls and gaudy sages,
somewhere in the emerald rust of copper shingles.

The last stop.
Back to the station, to life.
Leave the Ping Shan Trail as an after-thought.

Nestled in hills
even I won't recall myself,
given time, and the
usual uncaring.

Kuk Po

Jennifer Lee Tsai

Plum blossom, peonies. I carry them to your house
on my back, uprooted flowers – I'm bent double with their weight.

My grandmother's village is far from here.
A forgotten ghost town, south of the Starling inlet.

I see the village through a screen.
Empty houses, the painted walls abraded by time.

Dusty furniture, random chairs and tables,
A mechanical, broken fan; abandoned tea ceremony.

Cows, chickens, pigs roamed in the fields.
Now only the cows are left;

wandering forlorn through the valley,
the occasional feral cat stalks the backstreets.

Wild vegetation sprawls over the farmland.
Still, some houses have running water

and electricity though no one lives there;
the owners have long emigrated abroad.

My grandmother's village is far from here
If you go there, you won't see a soul.

I went there once in another time; their house
had darkened to an unholy glow, lit only

by the shadow of the moon; she was alive,
greeted me with open arms but grandfather cast me aside.

Ngee Sik Ng Sik

Roland Tsoi

No one ever tells you how easily a language dies;
it melts into the skin, dead cells flake through the air
as it is denied passage onto another generation.
Hakka, her words of a guest family moulding like the folds of her
elderly skin.

It's said that with time,
the blood has difficulty breaking down the sugar;
The sucrose crystallises in the bloodstream,
depositing particles on the estuary.

The sweetness of her smile fades,
as she comes and goes out of consciousness.

My aunt peels an orange, a colour radiant.
Sunshine in her hands.
My grandmother's eyes tremor as she wakes.
The wedge is placed between her lips, her face contort into itself;
wrinkling lines that converge onto her nose.
Muscles fight against the tears that swell until her eyes turn red.
Her gums mash words.
"*Haó Sûen*".

In the silence, I dig up the words in a language I do not know well.
"*Mao tong mah?*"

She groans at the bland meal,
My aunt has smuggled some soy sauce.
Small pleasures
amongst the pastel walls and vacant stares from passers by.

Her eyes droop
"*Koi m koi ah?*" I ask
"*Hao koi*" she answers.

She struggles to keep her eyes open,
her head nestled on a mountain of pillows.

Cantonese

Chris Tse

如果同一個人用佢識嘅語言溝通，佢會聽入腦。
如果用佢自己嘅語言同佢嚟溝通，佢就會聽入心。

If you talk to a man in a language he understands, that goes to his head.
If you talk to him in his own language, that goes to his heart.

The list of topics in which I can have conversations with my Dad
in Cantonese   shrinks with each passing year.   I can ask him

how to steam egg to the perfect silky consistency.   I can tell him
I'm too busy to visit because I have a poem to write. He can share

his regrets with me, but I can't offer comfort back to him in his first
tongue.   I can only nod to show that I understand.   The limits

of your language define the limits of your world.   In the world
I share with my Dad   we're both on the side lines expecting

each other to leap onto the court with effortless words to play
a syncopated game.   Instead we fault ourselves in two languages

and I hear the hesitation in his voice when he switches to English
because we've reached an impasse.   In these moments

my biggest regret is not having done enough to speak to his heart.
Even this poem won't make a difference. Even this poem is a wall.

Lotus Flower Kingdom

Stephanie Chang

after Ren Hang

Sunday catch. I do the honors. I harvest the lily pads.

The lily pads exploding like funguses. They break the surface tension.

Between your breasts. Redswim and gunblot.

Outside the soldiers shoot swans up against glass.

Hands up. Hot resin. Let the windows petrify their shape into
permanence.

I clean the shit blemished at the bottom of the Dim Sum fish tank.

I am paid in fox-thieved pulses. I tempt life to lust after me.

A daughter is best described not as the object

of desire but the verb. The kingdom has a capital

punishment worse than death. Pelted bones. When the body is
bludgeoned

to nothing but its desires. Organs crying cellophane. The Dim Sum
ladies

gossip about my father. Call him a public menace. Made of the sport

of swans. Verdant tongue. He was found dead in a fish tank.
Unbearable

lotus flower, he would say, sopping in shit, we are not so lucky

this time. The first time I loved someone. I thought I was ready to die.

Hours piling on hours. I swallowed. Ginkgo leaves. Bit the heads

off orchids. Monkey face. Moth. Boat flower. Traded nipples for pistils.

Violets to violence to violence. I dreamt of threading my spine
through the eye

of a storm. My hands thunderstruck into salute.
When I woke I had already been playing dead for so long
I became a kingdom of flowers and a kingdom of fangs.
I jester. I the king of my own perfect crime. I flower to no end.

Triple Sonnet for Veronica Lodge's Tigers

Dorothy Chan

There are too many poems about fathers.
Or not enough. I used to hate mine until
I remembered the fortune teller's theory
that my father and I are symbols of each
other—maybe this is why in my dreams
I say goodbye to him last whenever
I go on a mission across the river—We're
a Tiger Father and a Snake Daughter who
aren't supposed to get along, the insistence
of tigers that they're the leaders of the zodiac—
the secrecy of snakes, like how the idea of
living a discreet life resonates so much with
queer little me. A lover asks if my father
knows that I've kissed girls. I tell him that

men don't need to know everything. Tiger Dads
always do the most—or is the magical four
letter word actually *best* in this case. As a child,
I took home the gold from math competitions:
use the four numbers on the card to create 24—
I'd watch other children cry when they lost
their rounds, stoic little me staring at their tears,
their mothers hugging them, saying they could
now leave and go to McDonald's. How sad it is
to lose and eat McNuggets, is a feeling I'll never
know, because my dad was always the last person
I said goodbye to before rounds—my lucky symbol,
two rivers cross—I don't want to get all Freud,
but my mother and I get along better in life,

*

while my father and I get along better in dreams,
both real and imagined. In Kowloon, he takes me
to the McDonald's where he won a gold pen
when he was a young man. Tiger Dads only breed
winners, and more stories where I inherit qualities
from my dad: his high alcohol tolerance, his habit
of four hours of sleep per night, the assumption of
authority everywhere I go—the raw ambition,
and I feel like Veronica Lodge in the episode
when she visits the guidance counsellor who tells her
that Veronica and her father are parallels of each
other. Like Veronica, I'm the desirable girl walking
around like I own the place, whose father would buy
me a baby tiger if he could—pushing me to win at life.

Madame X

Jessica Chan

if they see you now
not boy not girl your chest
pressed flat as the sheets
maybe they will forgive us
our skittish romance,

our devilish tangling
pass the salt, i grow
hungrier still, the cage
shifts restless near my horns.
your rhinestone strap drops

chase the golden apples
but run faster back
before the gates close and
the lions unwrap you
here take my hand

hopscotch lovers see your
pink ear in my mouth
maybe we are just best friends
when we roll eyeballs down
burning salty pavements

maybe they will listen next year
or the next or maybe a century
later i will wear my ring and
you will wear yours and they
will not be the same they will

call us silly call us witches
either way my fingers press against
your sweaty thighs and you scream
curses for this burning city do not
look back, the ferry slicing the dirty water.

‘Hoping’ by Leung

THREE

'The winner in the winner's circle is
always the circle itself'

('Soft Tank', James Shea)

Reading Louise Ho on the MTR

Michael Tsang

On a sardine-packed MTR train at Tsim Sha Tsui, I was standing in front of a young couple, Louise Ho's *Incense Tree* in hand. I read her for research, this poet who hesitated at being called a 'Hong Kong poet.' The couple was sitting next to the train door, but after a while, out of the corner of my eye I caught the guy sinking his neck into his body, one-fifth of an inch at a time, as if testing whether he's capable of enterology. Then his neck re-emerged and he mumbled something to the girl. She similarly contorted and mouthed something in return.

Everything was done "undercover," like some immoral act. Who knows, reading could be an immoral act in this city now. I could have looked up from the poem "Home to Hong Kong" and murdered their curiosity with daggers from my eyes. Instead, I tilted the book up ever so slightly so that more light could illuminate the shadowed jacket.

Perhaps their attention was arrested by the book's refreshingly green cover amidst a sea of smartphones. When everyone is so immersed in their retina screens nowadays, reading a paperback in public—not to mention a poetry volume, if they still exist—is a spectacle inviting scopophilia like a polar bear in a tropical zoo.

That was when I sensed the middle-aged couple standing behind me also snooping at the pages. We have all had that experience of swaying left to right, forward and backward, when the train was speeding unsteadily. But you always know when someone is leaning a bit too close to you. Maybe they were drawn to the words "Hong Kong Riots" because they had also "stood / upon others' shoulders / plastering posters / outside / the Governor's house."

I flipped a page and could feel their bodies tense up at the date June 4th, 1989. I moved the book farther from me so that my head wasn't blocking their view. The gentleman made a cough, the lady drew a sharp breath. I hoped they would not forget that they had once stormed on the "rock bottom of a totalitarian state," and twenty-five years later we did the same.

Or did the younger couple really do that? The guy had a huge plush toy on his lap. I bet they had never heard of Louise Ho before, or for that matter, they never knew there were even poets in Hong Kong, let alone writing in English. Now they were looking back and forth at my book and each other. I had no time to talk through my research. Maybe I could just bellow: Louise Ho *is* a Hong Kong poet.

The train reached Admiralty. Their curiosity only lasted for a cross-harbour journey. Then everything happened in a split second: the middle-aged couple moved to the door while the young people stood up. Just as I slipped into a seat and was about to geeleegulu with Ho, I could hear the girl's high-pitched voice: *dào le ma?*

請勿靠近車門

Kika Man

Please move away from the doors. I leap, take a seat, look up at all the not so elderly people, and wonder if I am in my right. Look at me, tell me you want this seat. Why do your bulging eyes not talk? Can I stay? My uncertainty keeps me frozen to my seat. I am a frog shut underwater while the ice starts to crack. Spring is almost over but global warming rendered this tropical greenhouse into a chilled winter garden. The A/C blows – I melt onto the floor. Puddle out the doors, my most secret core leaks onto the tracks. And the people walk, they sneer, they glide over my intestines. I do not perish. I evaporate and leave the station along with the steam escaping through the vents. Long have I gone from materialising, there's no turning back now. Don't take their seats. Stand up for yourself. I am everywhere.

Essay on Stochasticity

Marco Yan

Instead of seeking luminosity in words, I watch the afternoon
stagnate on a red wall.

Outside, cardboard boxes, bamboos for scaffolding strewn on the
floor, all glistening.

More than a reprieve from heat, more than an enchantment, the
storm has transformed the swath of Mongkok.

Overwhelming the road, rain pours into the gutter, which at first is
clear, then a flow of dirt.

The man I loved grew tired of this peninsula and left me for the
Greek mountains, the grayness of wandering.

Why am I surprised?

Goodbye gust, goodbye to the bird who sees my mountains as hills.

I want to know how two leaves stay afloat together when the river
keeps debouching into the sea.

Somewhere in the Pacific, a humpback whale is falling, deep blue
rising to fill the absence.

There's so much moisture in the air the neighborhood is shrouded
in mist.

And silence too, so I decide the cricket on the ledge is clicking for
me, thinking of me.

Perhaps this is the city's last idyll: a crack on the window, refracted
light,

condensation, a screw below the light switch rusting away—

to see in the disarray a glimmer and abide this order of things.

The Slice, the Bus and the Astronaut
Atom Cheung

The Slice

Skilled at avoiding the slice, a moth taunts the blades of a ceiling fan. No one's ever flown through and come back, says the chalk's tick-tacking against the board. A pen case is dented and picked up. I'm drawn, more to the art of fluttering than staying intact.

Clear windows. Orbiting dust. The day lets itself onto the floor, splitting truths from guesses. The legs of chairs and desks sparkle, and also the backs of polished leather shoes. Words locked by the shoulders push against her forehead. A patch of morning finds her long strands, its ends grazing the sheets laid flat and the cursives that slant to the left.

The Bus

Upper deck. The two of us. The bus lulled to a stop. The width of the plaza and its vaporous lampposts fit perfectly through the window. I said I liked the red lights more than the green and she said she liked them both and – completely blindsided – our bodies flung against the hard backs of the seats in front of us.

The dream contains a bruise the size of a punctured lung. A rusted door sealed tight, its hinges discoloured by rotting from the inside out. A sickening symmetry that triggers something sharp, protruding from the unbroken knuckles of my right hand.

The Astronaut

The astronaut's perspective on, and positioning relative to, the subject being written about has never been more reliable. From the back corner of the sky, one sees everything. Detachment is futile.

I will eat you, she says. And I'd be writing about her process of deciding when and how to have me devoured, and whether that were to happen at all, and in what direction, along the subject-object sequence, the devouring was to occur.

Texaco Road

Cass Donnelly

—and the greyness threatens the leaves,
who shed themselves, fearing erosion,
preferring to land in their graves as they were,
and the pale light slides along dry tile,
and the rainwater eats light and shadow—

—and i retire, to play with sand, digging
gleefully amongst the bones of my betters,
heedlessly letting it run out of my hand,
letting it slip between flowers of denim and rayon,
letting it shore up the putrid ship docks—

—and it is hot again, cold again, hot again,
and I mark my days with permutations of the closet,
stake out my almanac with stale recipes,
and wonder flatly at my wonder,
and flip the eternal hourglass sideways—

—and peddle my hours, sterile, empty,
trade meaning to extend infinity,
and think it incredible! a bargain,
to find immortality, stretched and stale,
smeared onto an noncommittal sky—

—and if i live, somewhat, somehow,
swept along the stairs with rainwater and foliage,
and block out damp shuffling with noise cancelling,
and clutch, wary of chance, the rails—

—and stare, uncomprehending, at the busker.
Briefly, everything is beautiful, beatific,
A monument of uncompensated meaning
Beating ceaselessly against tedium.
and i am borne inexorably into the present—

Witness
Nicolette Wong

A nightly occurrence: the rain jabs at the crusty paints that have spurted across my balcony from moist rural heat. I have given up sweeping the tree leaves, paper scraps, and insect carcasses that land on the floor tiles amidst incessant winds. Dryness will come when the season is drained. When the flight halts in crisp, thready breaths that I let out at the periphery of home.

An artist I like once told me: he tried eating a ball of dust when he was a child. He said it tasted like marshmallows.

Dough

Ethan Luk

In the wet market,
the workers' hands are rough with
calluses— blisters

like ink blots of time.
I am an ink blot, too, when
my dead grandfather

gazes at me from
a casino in the sky,
wins all the money

he lost on this Earth.
Through a slot machine, he sees
me, running around

new cities, in search
of a temporary home
for my twenties.

In parallel time,
I live, he gambles. We are
united by our

waiting. I complain
Nothing's Happening. Same Here.
My grandfather moans.

I kissed a stranger,
but it felt like nothingness.
Should I give up love?

I ask. You can try,
but even in this wretched
casino, I mourn

I haven't loved you
enough. So what is enough?
The vegetables

in the wet market.
If I can leave this wretched
casino, I'll build

a house out of pork
and chives for you. You will laugh
till perilla leaves

fall out of your mouth.
You'll laugh at how dough means both
American cash

And smooth dumpling skin.
I'll walk out of this wretched
casino one day.

We'll meet in the house.
We will laugh till you forget
I even left you.

Dealing in Numbers

Kavita A. Jindal

This is an unlucky number
It has an unfortunate sound
The same as death
Yes, possibly yours.

I'm not superstitious
It's a connotation that's all
Yet I won't carry
Four notes in my wallet.

Four coins, four dollars, four pounds
four pence, four renminbi
I won't order four desserts
Or plant four trees.

Despite the last supper
Thirteen is my lucky number
It doesn't appeal to most
I step forward to claim it.

Adopting this with zeal
I lived for years at No. 13
In Chung Hom Kok;
I'm not superstitious.

So why not 4?
Wait a moment
In numerology
13 *is* 4.

Oh no.
Say eight quick.
Say seven, say nine. Drop a line.

After-school Snack

Silvia Tse

North Point is never in North Point
but the best egg bubbles travel
on steel pedals
or under a bridge, joining
Tuen Mun with Mong Kok.
Monday, half six
after work, nocturnal birds swoop in for
edible flames in a brown paper frock:

Star-studded crispy sheet,
soft pockets of steam.
Tofu, offals, peelables; shiny,
roasted pebbles in mahogany.

I guzzle the world my mother deems
'The Sheet of the Impure and Unclean'.
They don't have real kitchens, she says,
having never seen the magic weaving
between slotted spoons and neon yarn balls
dyed in ten curry sauces and one big pot
rolling with spiced tongues.

Be back by seven,
but I won't leave heaven till I breathe
chilli oil as the
Chinese band trumpets
static on the makeshift telly —
[somewhere my father drinks] Sugar
leung caa ci, [A whistle, black flags]
A smidgen of dried orange peel. *

Today I will be home
eating with chopsticks as we watch
The Salting n' Peppering of Soy Street.
I'll question my mother, a cordon bleu,
one last time, if she knew vendors, too,
season their waffle pans on-the-run
with gases that remind them of onions;
if skin puffs up like fried tofu
when smoked in mace:
these delicacies in Portland Street. Will
eyes, like eggs,
jump when pierced
like boils on bubble wrap?
For the fourth time, my mother denies me
her recipes for Molotov tea.
My mother's father fought at Sha Tau Kok;
nowadays, she won't let me
drive near sports stadiums anymore,
or fire fishballs fished from brown paper bags.

---

* Sugar/ Leung cha ci: Chinglish and Cantonese romanization of 糖呢就兩茶匙, which directly translates to "two teaspoons of sugar". The phrase is directly taken from a PSA by the Broadcasting Authority, 'Share the joy of watching TV and provide children with guidance'. The dialogue from which the poem extracts, shows a housewife watching the television as she bakes, as the television voiceovers:「雞蛋六隻，糖呢就兩茶匙，仲有啲橙皮添」("six eggs, two teaspoons of sugar, plus a handful of orange zest").

A Father and Son in Rags, Downtown Hong Kong

John Wall Barger

They squat side by side
on a busy sidewalk, in front of a McDonald's
handing a hamburger back and forth,

each taking bites. The boy seems unaware
his father's hand is on his shoulder.
It's always been there.

Tourists and business people gush past,
riotous current. The boy says something
in his father's ear. The father, chewing,

thinks it over a long time.
This makes me love him. As an answer
he makes a sweeping gesture

with the burger, as if to suggest a vast world
beyond the bank towers,
beyond the cemeteries of taxis

and the ceaseless rain and smog
and gasoline rainbows, a world
where kindness begets kindness

and maybe a farm with a goat
grazing for a thousand years.
The boy nods, frowning.

Checherella

Cecil C. Elleran

Saturday night almost gone,
She piles the plates back when they're done.
Floor is gleaming, ironed clothes hung.
Status update: "Tomorrow will be fun."
Turns on tap, then starts singing,
Washes away six days of pain.
Her legs are sore, her back aching.
They're nursed in the warm shower rain.
She crawls to bed hugging the linen,
Teary eyes glued to a picture frame.
Next morning polished nails are glimmering,
Pouting lips carefully outlined.
Long back hair dangles a ponytail,
Skimpy tube on top a miniskirt.
She grabs a fancy Gucci bag,
Pointy stilettos crackle out loud.
Victoria's Secret perfume she sprays,
Sways her hips out the metal gate.
Breathing the air of Sunday freedom,
She scans the sea of foreign faces.
Amid shiny sunglasses, shoulder pats and kisses,
An inviting dancefloor gladly sits.
She lets loose, she rules the world.
With loud laughter the party booms.
Pair of strong arms wrap her waist,
To the dark corner they embrace.
She fools a guy with no disgrace,
Tells him she's Ana, Ruth or Carla.

By none of those names is she known,
Only a sweet loving *che che (tse tse)* back home.
Clock pointing to half past eight,
Heart beats fast, can't be late.
She washes the paint of masquerade.
Sunday night's over, another week awaits.

Your Room

Janet Bi Li Chan

Noise is not noise when you live with too many
people on the same floor. People in your room.
People in the other rooms. Workers who come
by during the day. Doing laundry, printing, talking.
Sound is all around you but you don't hear noise.
You sleep in the same room as your mother,

your sister, Ah Sun, who works with your mother,
and her daughter Ah Siu. You are luckier than many
who live in rooming-house bunks drowned in noise
of clattering clogs and screaming kids. Your room
is where you eat, sleep, listen to adults talking.
It's where you daydream, watch people come

and go. The window is the TV before TVs come
to homes. Out there is another world, your mother
and the room are left behind. A maître d' is talking
in a hushed voice. Gentlemen lead ladies with many-
jeweled chains into a chandeliered dining room
with plush carpet, away from the street noise.

This room is filled with sweet music, the only noise
the clinking of glasses. A sudden clank and you come
to your senses. You are back in your ragged room—
worn armchairs, iron bunk beds, and your mother
struggling to carry a heavy pot to the table. How many
more years, you wonder, can she keep working, talking

down her illness, hiding her surgery pain, still talking
of sending you to university? If cancer could make noise
this room would be rocking, this earth broken into many
shards. You never even thought the day might come
when this room will no longer be yours; your mother,
your sister and you will be hunting for another room,

a space for a dying woman and her children, a room
just big enough for a bunk and a table. No one's talking
about the rent that eats up your sister's pay. Your mother
is given a bag of pain-killers by a doctor. The only noise
you can make is silence. Sixteen years of service have come
to almost nothing. Just be glad that you've had many

perks because your mother was more special than many.
You may be surrounded by noise but you have a room.
Stop talking of injustice, look how far you have come.

Reflection

Nicholas Wong

after Mirror's "Innerspace"

Name one loop you currently are
stuck in. Be honest, do you, however
slightly, have anything to do
with it? Name one thing wondrous
that has happened to your body.
Are you a homely or outdoor kind
of person? Is daydreaming art
or science to you? Which Doraemon
gadget do you like best? What will
you do with it? Relate a giant uvula
to a natural happening.
Time your longest and shortest breath.
Average out the data. That's the length
of your esophagus. Where else,
if not the sky, do you think you would find
stars? What else, if not plants, hides
inside a glass house? Turn your spine
into a metaphor. Give an emotion noun
to your knees. Hold your body still
for a minute. What are the three words
in your mind? Invent a name
for your own DNA sequencing.
Is your life fiction, poetry, or a pantomime?
And what animal is likely its reader?

Rare on the Market

Peter Kennedy

Extremely exclusive in luxury verdant location,
this desirable property boasts breath-taking sea views,
is newly renovated, located on a single plot number with
permission pending for future triplex development.

Meticulously designed, it showcases contemporary Chinese décor:
zhennan and zelkova wood panels with pink taffeta and purple velvet
furnishings for a comfortable, modern, welcoming feel.
Though compact - saleable area, 28 by 30 by 78 - the practical layout

and impressive efficiency ratio makes it seem surprisingly spacious.
In a tranquil setting within private walls and en-suite - price inclusive
of security.
It boasts a lavish long lease without the usual six-year expiry date; it
is most
convenient for transport as well as club house facilities for Ching
Ming visitors.

Notes: A private burial plot in Hong Kong is rare and can easily cost HK$5 million dollars. A public grave costs HK$4,000 and can be "leased" for only six years. After that the remains are exhumed and cremated. The ashes are put in a columbarium or otherwise disposed of. Ching Ming (or 'grave sweeping' day) is when relatives pay their respects to dead relatives. Zhennan and zelkova wood are used to make Chinese coffins.

Soft Tank

James Shea

I dub everything in my own voice.

My mouth never matches perfectly with what I am saying.

I'm sorry.

Life can be life-like, if you like life.

The winner in the winner's circle is always the circle itself.

Can't see that star in the sky?

It's like someone left a flashlight on in the bottom drawer.

Last night, it rained inside a mall.

There's very little crime here, but there could be a war.

‘Universe’ by Yvette Chan

FOUR

'Like a war in the stars making noise
we can't hear'

('There Is a Season Waiting Behind This One',
Collier Nogues)

There Is a Season Waiting Behind This One

Collier Nogues

This morning began with soldiering. A battle, some heroism
I dreamed myself into,
                                        out of these vague days become pure
routine. I led a drill no one wanted to follow, convinced no one,
even with real fire behind us smoking up the horizon

beyond which our sincerest hopes,
beloved, backed down again.
                                                  The radio switched on and off without
our touching it. What came over the air was someone else's
war, or it was ours we began to make out in the purple blossoms
blooming,
            the red blooms waning over the public
pool backed by the factory block.
The river's its own gauge;
                            it's full as can be. It smells like a new town
the night a single law arrives to carry all of us,our children,
our animals forward.
            One animal, left, lifts her nose to the air.
                                                    A war of language,
like a sea war, like a drone war, like
a war in the stars making noise we can't hear
though the drones are made where we live, their noise so close,
their superhighway
                            entirely lit, blinking
into dusk, the yellowjackets swirling in a fog
around the flowers.

Not one of us could turn the corner as easily as that. Not one of us owns
our own home or hopes to.
                                        The police ask a man wearing black for his wallet.
The police walk around in fatigues.
No bloom looks the same to me under this sky
if I can see the sky, if it's the kind of sky that's visible
above my government.
                                        What light it sheds I try to follow
into night and out again, surrounded
by fellow citizens. I wave to them.

The nearest ones wave back, then look straight up,
setting down their well-worn umbrellas now that umbrellas
are no longer of use.
                            Looking straight up, you have to
open your eyes to see the clouds moving
another direction than what you'd expected. You have to keep your
            eyes open
even as rain fills up their wells.

Admiralty

Shirley Geok-lin Lim

(2014, 2019)

Five years have passed, five long years, and still
planes land and lift off the tarmac, hills
not yet dwarfed by thickening towers
filling up and emptying of people,
fixed unstable on sea and land however
mixed.
          Five years and still the children's chants
echo in the millions' multi-level haunts.
Its canyons' windows open to grannies
watchful of children's children, the city's
uncles, grandpas in wheelchairs, the aunts
who had been only girls five years ago.

Two million on the march is slow
motion exercise of a people's will.
Avenues in black, in black and white: what ills
occupy the world's channels? Their mono-
chrome of grief is grievance against tomorrow's
losses.
          Their bosses' gambles are sorrow
sowed in a wind not of their election.
The young sing in English elocution,
rally in Cantonese, day-dream horror
sci-fi future worlds.
                              Five years have passed,
each year in Hong Kong, someone's last.

The Tomorrowless People

Wendelin Law

watching, as the ravening gyres scourged
the spreading fire and all that met the eyes.

Burning took hold; burning was how to hold
shadows back from swallowing each other.

Black flags whacked, whacked by raging gas--trailing
blazes--white projectile tails--a descending tyranny

of dread. Watching, as tears streaked down the sky.
Still watching, as the sun was hatched from dying fire:

the morning was weightless. You leave or you stay.
The world is never loveless. You burn or you burn.

Quiet. The tomorrowless people. Crawling
in sewers, they tried to salvage the last of days.

But shadows pursued. Their maws snapped
as the day collapsed. Their grip only tightened

while watching, the pyres of universities--
the embers of all our tomorrows--whipped

and thrashed--as the pandemonium danced
in gyres and gyres. Only ashes would remember.

What the Mother Cannot Say

Andrew Barker

What's heard within these walls where we don't speak
For fear of what our words would then make real?
It starts with gestures, looks, then week by week
You learn how much a silence can reveal.
Her shopping trips, the rain that makes her weep,
The clothes she wears home sometimes aren't the same
As those she left in. When I watch her sleep,
I see my baby daughter once again.
And I see him, so angry and confused;
His television scaring him, each night
Of watching, hoping she won't be there too:
His wonder that she might be in the right.
    How close they were surviving without me,
    Each other as their only company.

Magpie Robin

Agnes Lam

Sunday –

I met
a magpie robin,

soft black,
a white breast,
stripes on its wings,
its tail held high,

hopping light
with no fear
a few feet
before me,

leading all the way
up the steep slope ...

– across the harbour,
Mongkok MTR exits
were charred by petrol fires
the night before –

... I went on walking
some paces behind
my magpie robin
this autumn morning

till before the steps
of my church,

it flew into the sky ...

Term of Art

Henry Wei Leung

Whereas helicopters keep shoveling above us
out of sight; *whereas* streetposts scan for objects
among persons, longing to see our hair, our masks,
untied; *whereas* for us the unmasking means
being faceless again in a small box of a city
where the most exotic myth was home; *whereas*
to live seven million strong in the box
was to rage at the season's arrival of typhoon
and tyrant; *whereas* our towers grow down now,
underground; *whereas* the slow-motion violence
of our parents' keeping their heads down
left us nothing but the edge of the sea; *whereas*
however we sliced it, the waves kept rising;

determining that the next wave always rises;
uncertain you'll recognize me after all this salt,
sickness, lying in state; *recognizing* there is
no antidote to sovereignty; *afraid* of state;
afraid of self; *determined* to lose only one
or the other; *and imagining* meanwhile
a future for us romantic rats, us savagely
kind roaches, in a world less and less
human, a world lately burning; *therefore*

I hold: how hollow to leave, free,
for a place not of one's choosing,
to be soluble, sea-swept, cloaked
by a map in which all roads
are removed—like a flag—
I hold myself like a flag.

Scared

Tammy Lai-Ming Ho

My poems are scared
of shapes that stand out.
All my lines lean neatly
on the left margin.
They are scared of visual
gaps, maps, and wilful
blending of doing and being.
Scared of illusions of saying
enough or too little. Of life.
Of course, of death.

The Last Words of a Dying Girl

Swann Adara Lee

i think the sun is setting, and its golden yolk
is trickling down my swollen throat,
the last thing i will ever eat and ever taste.
i think the sun is setting, and it hurts,
because i downed it in a shotglass
and spat it in my best friend's face before
he left me to die in this grey, grey city.
i am grey too, and i will be grey after i am
lowered in the ground, but i know there
were other colours before that i shoved
into my sickly sweet mouth and slurped
down before they could tell me to stop.
i cannot even feel how much it hurts,
this foreign lump of light i have consumed
that cannot weep for me. please tell the
hills i loved to hike that i will take
their shape, and the old man down at
the *cha chaan teng* that i loved his daughter
once, and that cantonese syllables no
longer feel so strange to me as my own
mother's breast.

Butterflies of Hong Kong

Neil Martin

A million butterflies have landed in the city,
lighting up the spaces no one's Instagrammed:

a flare in the underpass, a gloaming in Tai Po,
a kaleidoscope spinning around a concrete stairwell.

Subversive lepidopterists have set them here
like Post-it notes on shop windows and walls.

No use thinking you'll understand them any better
by studying their genus or knowing their Latin names.

Instead, look closer. See how their intricate patterns
articulate the things we cannot say: a thin calligraphy

of illicit speech, a palimpsest on papery membranes,
words written over each other to conceal our desires,

amplify our rage. O shimmer swarm, rainbow rabble:
why would you be here if not to bring us hope?

Days your heart hangs heavy as fog on the harbour,
go and read the poems on their luminous wings.

Moving Out at Night

Polly Ho

So hectic —
they knock around 12 a.m.
accompanied by the famous microbiologist
Professor Yuen.

You can't stay here tonight.
We suspect that the virus is coming into your house
through the sewage pipes in the bathroom.
You must move out for the sake of your health!

Holy cow!
Cries Mrs Lam,
who lives in Cheung Hong Estate
with her son and daughter-in-law.
She is 66, suffers diabetes, high-blood pressure,
liver disease
— prone to die if she contracts the virus.

She packs her essentials,
grabs the valuables and her gold teeth.

I don't understand,
Why don't they close the border,
give out masks and sanitizers?
What does the government do these days?
I can't buy toilet paper in the supermarket this week.
Now I have to leave my home in the middle of the night.
Where are you taking me now?

The Disease
Victoria Walvis

A Sai Kung Village

On sunlit days it's hard to believe we're dying.

Curtain rises on cancelled playdates,
unpaid leave, redundancies swelling
like the green squash.
Someone next door has it.

It's awkward now we sidestep on the path,
walking our dogs like excuses.
A man does rooftop callisthenics each dawn.
We read fiction and recipes for bread.
The news counts the dead.
Kids are confined to the trampoline
singing *Ring a Ring o' Roses*, irony
lost on pigtails and gingham dresses.
Dad cuts the fly-ridden tree and the chainsaw
coughs, roars, stops. *We all fall down.*

Then there's the story of a civet cat:
desperate and hungry, she follows
her head injury into our village.
The rangers take her away.
There are maggots in her brain.

Last act is an encore of tree crickets.
The forest draws back from lights
too weak to reach each other.

A constellation of islands in water so dark,
it must contain some sort of answer.

Twelve Ways of Looking at Blue
Florence Ng

Blue hits me with the newsfeed on my phone.
Blue vaporizes with my brewed coffee.

Blue hits me when a colleague resigns.
Blue dissolves as my cat rolls on his back.

Blue hits me when I'm queuing for the bus.
Blue makes way when I'm getting off.

Blue hits me when someone leaves the city.
Blue drowns in my favourite TV drama.

Blue hits me when everyone asks *Are you leaving.*
Blue sings aloud and loses itself in earphones.

Blue hits me in the face forcing me to look straight at it.
Blue lets go of me after I acknowledge it with a kiss.

Blue hits me with a text message.
Blue melts hot on French fries.

Blue hits me with my body in the mirror.
Blue smiles as my cat follows me to the bathroom.

Blue hits me with the same bland day.
Blue fades as I stroll into Emily Dickinson's forest.

Blue hits me when someone is crushed like an ant.

Blue breathes in, breathes out, thinking about nothing, nothing at all.

A Simple Destruction

WaWa

Day one: A blue pitcher plant arrived at my door.
I received it in my facial mask.

Day two: The plant crawled onto my bed
when I was sleeping with teddy.

Day three: Teddy dismantled. The plant, glued
to my face, has sucked out one of my eyeballs.

Day four: I fumbled about with one eye. No more
mosquitoes in my place. One pocket crept into my mouth.

Day five: Furniture shattered. Bedroom walls cracked open.
The blue plant started sinking into my face.

Day six: I walked into the bathroom, stared at the mirror,
put on another facial mask.

Day seven: A mail arrived at my door. I, wearing
a facial mask, am still beautiful.

Ghost Tigers

Portia Yu

Ghost tigers
with ghost stripes
stalk through streets
languid in the sunlight
their eyes are pits
they stop traffic with their breath
leave claw marks on pavements
and stains of death in every forgotten place

They smell like the rain
like the heaviness of stone
history bearing down on twigs
snapping
bones sinking in the mud

I did not always see them
years ago, I lived in ignorance
then one day
it was just a tiny scratch
right at the corner of my eye
I was sliced open
and afterwards I saw everything

I do not fear the tigers
I feed them with my words
they are fond of sentence fragments
and stories without endings
the tigers are starved

for things that need not die
they put their paws up on my shoulders, whine
I give them all that I can
not enough
my pupils are wide and theirs are wide
it is dark dark dark down here
it kills me every time.

Calling Home

Mary Jean Chan

after Anne Carson

While talking to your mother, you keep your fingers busy, your mind elsewhere. Her voice flows through your soul like air. You steady your voice, but she knows to ask about the tightness in your throat. After all that has happened, have you finally forgiven each other? The child asks: how long will it feel like burning. Your mother wants to know what you had for lunch, tells you what she ate for dinner. This mutual exchange of images. You ask her to turn on her camera so you can see her, knowing she will refuse. Another day, she says. How to tell her that after decades on earth, you should be able to know each other. That what children want is for their parents to see them, as they already are. Instead, you are sent photos of yourself: an eight-year-old in a beige dress at a wedding, an awkward teenager dressed for the opera in Milan on your first trip to Europe. How to tell her: none of those versions fit anymore. Your partner walks into the room. You are reminded that you cannot change those you love most, your voice blue in the violet hour.

'Untitled' by Tung Pang Lam

FIVE

'The small triumph in closing the distance between the body and what is outside of it'

('Fetch', Tammy Lai-Ming Ho)

Hoi Ha

Martin Alexander

Remember fireflies in that magic wood
Where finger-roots and tangled branches made
A ghostly cave, as dusk surrendered to
The dark? We'd left our Hoi Ha tent to sneak
With Toby down the village path to buy
Warm beer and cans of Coke. We wedged them tight
And cold among the stream's wild tumbled rocks
And shivered in the pool while Toby barked
And leaped at monsters in the dark. Our fire
Burned bright. I read aloud and then you slept.
We'd jumped the sand cliffs, swum the stream's wide mouth
And floated out into the scary deep.
  Later, as you dreamed, curled small and only
  Eleven, I stood outside and stared at stars.

Change with Constancy

Gillian Bickley

Goddess of the Sea, Tin Hau, speaks.

I have been here for a long long time
facing out to sea, protecting the villagers at Chek Lap Kok.

When the foreigners first came in their big sailing ships,
I was already here.

When the cannon sounded in the Tiger's Mouth
and the mandarins' power was challenged by the West,
I observed the outcome and the consequence
more ships that sailed the sea.

And now my villagers are moving me away
the men that fish my sea,
the women that mourn their men folk's loss
taking me with them to Tung Chung on Lantau,
where they also go.

I am wearing my silk robe, bordered with pearls, and
my head-dress also is bedecked with pearls.

Before boarding the boat, we take a last look
round the village, saying farewell. The people are
sad to leave. But the big machines that fly
need another place to land; and they want this place of ours.

As for us, the sea (not the sky) is our element. We can find
another place to merge with it, facing its bounties and banes.
The villagers have changed but not so much, that they
forget the ways their ancestors have followed.
The clothes they wear are sometimes foreign clothes;
but they eat the dishes that they always ate,
baak choi, choi sum, rice, fish and other vegetables.

The children learn both western knowledge
and our Chinese ways.

But their hearts are mine.

Rock

Laura Jane Lee

cursed
landscape,
little art. son
birth while sea
sleep.   myth weaver,
folk   fisher. breath
of nurs ing babe and
saltwater. snapped sail
boat, grave of sea. hill-
top vantage come waver hope.
senseless pilgrimage then shore
afar. sun & wind & rain & time.
miserable faith. till month till
year. truthblind. perhaps love.
then. thunder trip, storm light.
cease to be. both. nothing. tear.
heaven pity, mortal fate. creation.
little legend. figure. & mother & child.
jagged form. wish of grief, eternal pine.
keep small watch, and wait, and wait.

The Shopping Cart

Henrik Hoeg

In the poems I studied at school
The tides were the interminable force
Promising to swallow the land eventually
All would be again a primal sea
It isn't so
There's a spot where the water used to begin
Where we stood once together
And threw a shopping cart into the harbor
I pushed it while you sat inside
Through the small hours
Further than made any sense
You had been down
Heartbreak, if memory serves
It's always heartbreak
I remember the muted splash
The emotional release that comes
With a well punctuated ending
That spot now is surrounded
On all sides
With buildings already considered old
By the city's warped timescale
The city, like a hummingbird
Living so fast the world appears in slow motion
Determined metabolism eyeing the ocean
Turning sustenance to energy and entropy
Reclaiming land that was never ours
Slowing down became the enemy
But I don't see the world like that

Sometimes I can still stand on that spot
Surrounded by concrete and noise
And look down at the sidewalk and see the ocean
And hear the splash of the shopping cart
Before it disappears into oblivion

Fetch

Tammy Lai-Ming Ho

I've grown tired of aquatic metaphors,
especially those about my city.
The other morning I saw a dog in the sea
excited to swim far out again and again

to retrieve a toy bone thrown
by its absent-minded owner next to the shark
lines. Was it the fake chewed bone?
The freedom of movement

in water? The familiarity of the routine?
The small triumph in closing the distance
between the body and what is outside
of it? I can't interrogate what prompts

joy in dogs or fish, but I remember
that whole moment and me in it—
becoming an agentless metaphor.
To thine own happiness be too.

Star Struck

David McKirdy

Star struck tourists
cliché their way across the harbour
in kitsch historic style
having scanned the brochures
and watched Nancy Kwan as Suzie Wong
sashay across the gangway.

But 50 years ago
Nancy Kwan as Nancy Kwan
travelled to and fro
there and back with the rest of us.
Downstairs for the unwashed masses
delivery bicycles with baskets of live chickens
British schoolboys
with long hair and a twenty-a-day habit
upstairs in first for the rest.

A burnished brass plaque declares:
'Hull built and machinery installed by
The Hong Kong and Whampoa Dock Company.'
My father built these vessels.
Northern Star, Night Star, Day Star
each one contains his essence
Shining Star, Twinkling Star
paid our school fees
Morning Star, Silver Star
put food on the table.

*

A Hong Kong icon
founded by Parsee merchants
designed by British shipwrights
Built and crewed by Chinese working men.
The short trip between Island and Mainland
once a lifeline
now the tee-shirt experience
of a package tour
in our world city.

So government pragmatists moved the pier
surprised by a riot of protest -
the ghostly reminder
of bloodlines drawn in sand
the collective memory of a city divided
by race, ideology and fortune.

For years
governments have failed to listen.

It's our city
our heritage
our history.

Listen now.

At the Market Butcher in Tai Po

John Wall Barger

At the market butcher
a metal cage twists with existence.
It is a mass of frogs
climbing each other,
mouths grave and comical,
eyes bugging out.
A little hell worthy of Bosch.
They make fancy dishes:
legs cooked in soy sauce,
served with garlic.
Each the price of a pack
of gum. I buy one, a baseball
of fat, bracing himself
inside the plastic bag
with his weird suction cup hands
like a TV superhero
in deep trouble
before we cut to commercial.
Under a nearby bridge
I let him hop out.
I've seen frogs here
staring at the river
like old sailors. Away he hops
onto the highway.

Cycling to Tai Mei Tuk

Jason Eng Hun Lee

Here at last you arrive at the world's end
where the bay parts to admit the water—

and with twilight still ahead you lift your foot
off the pedals to wonder at the sun's last triumphal arch.

What is life but a rolling world of motion? Behind you,
Kwan Yin stands—Goddess of Mercy—a distant shadow.

Ahead, no more hazardous roads, just that
single proverbial light after a journey. Look

how the path juts straight into that place where sea meets sky—
the azure depths rising to gold, a heavenly mirage!

On either side the wheat sheaves dip effortlessly
to embrace the rocks, the shoreline, calling you to them.

And so with each temporary solace
you feel your tumultuous desires fade,

seeing the pleasure barges and pedal boats lapping idly,
the fisherfolk rising jovially from their task.

Affectionate couples wander arm-in-arm still,
an early glint of Spring in their eyes perhaps,

or the promise of your own self, awakened once more,
like a kite that pulls you off your habitual feet, into air.

You stare out at that wistful landscape, recalling all
that you've given up, what you'll give up still

and just as you turn back home, so another boy,
one like you, puts his short legs to the wheel

to race out of you, out of your sight, back
towards the horizon, to where you first began.

How to Make a Mixed Baby

Chioma Onuoha

Prep time: 9 months
Cook time: For eternity, or until it dies
Servings: Serves you and your spouse indefinitely

Ingredients:
5 tbsp of Christianity
A slice of an overworked mother
A squeeze of lemon
1 mid-sized apartment
A dash of a neglectful father
A pinch of curly hair

Instructions:
1. Mother should drink this soup daily till the baby appears 9 months later.
2. Don't act surprised when it turns out to be a girl.
3. Pour the child into a school (the international type, the chase-your-dreams-but-don't-wander-too-far type).
4. Place over a Christian guilt stove. Proceed to whip until steam cries out of the soup.
5. Make sure to spot for bits of scrumptious creativity and pluck out to not spoil the child.
6. Squash pieces of defiance to make the soup finer, more submissive to taste (according to preference).
7. Serve in a jar. Close the lid and place it on a shelf until it starts to bloom.
8. When the smell starts to permeate the house, throw the jar out the door and hear its glassy innocence shatter into pieces.

9. Lock the door. Ignore (even when you hear sobbing).
10. Forget, rewind, walk out the door into shards of glass and now you're bleeding.

Babysitting in Ho Man Tin

Ian Humphreys

I walk into my bachelor pad and see an ape
hanging from the ceiling light, swinging
round and round with a nappy on his head.
He shrieks and leaps into my arms. For seven days,
this month-old Cambodian gibbon, unshackled
from the black market, adopts me as his city mother.

He eats only grapes, bites the kitten's paws.
At night, his liana limbs entwine my neck.
Each breath, a swallowtail flutter. Disposable
wipes keep him dry and I soothe chafed legs
with palm oil lotion. Months after he's rehomed,
I crazydream of giant safety-pins and a baby

dangling from the jungle canopy, his real mother
reaching out, unable to touch her child. He turns to her
but his face is my face. Our umbilical cord snakes
into the red gape of a pitcher plant. In a blink,
I'm swaddled in cotton, pram, England – awakening
under an ocean of sky. Looking up in wonder.

||: 碰 :||

Josephine Yip

|1. ________

is a mahjong move with a deeper lesson
you learn to make the most
out of what others leave you

|2. ________

is the merging of souls
you smile and are relieved that
someone else shares your thinking

|3. ________

is the physical sensation of a pat on your back
you receive their well intentions but extract
none of the comfort

|4. ________

is the sting in your knuckles
when you knock on wood
after saying *I'll get better, one day*

when you see the red stains on the wall from the
new year decorations you tore down, then knock
a little too hard so that your cup tips over

|5. ________

is when you bump into someone on the street
unexpectedly; you turn around and cup
your hands over your mouth ||

I still tremble from that memory

because 碰𝄐, or collision

is when you repeatedly encounter the shadow
of someone you cannot meet again
someplace you cannot return to

a long-forgotten spark
their influence always hanging
over you like the white-turned-yellow-over-time cotton blanket
you hang out to dry, full of scratches from when it snagged on
branches and bits of rock, and yet that is
the blanket you bury
your head into as you try
to sleep at night ||

Different Skin

Mags Webster

i.
at the rim
of a city, poached in smog,
rice paper screen of sky

coastlines are bespoke,
land rephrased,
post scriptum

the tides sculpt runes
of abandoned shoes,
rope ampersands
and plastic cups

spider-jointed
trawlers drag
the bays, scrape
absence from
their depths

ii.
here, where the cloud
emulsifies the sun

my lungs hoist
slackened flags,

make languid fans
for my heart's
dull coal, its shiver
of ash in rib-grate

iii.
I wear a different
skin, a humid lucence
sweats from pores

I'm steamed *har gau*,
an oyster tipped
from the slipper
of its shell,

glazed with the moist
veneer of heat
I understand what
mouthfeel means

as the famished air
digests me

iv.
in the shadow
of Lo Fu Tau
I try to open
the hand of thought

to winnow
the good grain
from the salt

I am the tree
where birds don't rest,
my roots unsure
how to grip this soil

v.

two kites coast white
space overhead, make
xíngshū with their wings

I have built a hide
of lotus leaf, wrapped
myself in hay

I must learn to erase
old scripts, sift new
words from the shoreline

Office

Eddie Tay

in your beige obedient room
 there's an elliptical shadow
and you know there's a giant billboard
 of running shoes and tanned athletes
and a brilliant logo on the glass
 of the opposite grey building
though there's nowhere to go from here
 you cower behind your desk
and put on trendy wireless earphones
 you say you've got ringing tinnitus and it's all ok
with men in suits and ties and women in scarves
 and you laugh quietly in time for lunchboxes
it's coffee and brown sugar
 and spreadsheets on your screen
and you laugh quietly and you know somewhere
 there're trees growing quietly green
making sense of the surrounding wild brown grass
 the grass will grow over and it's still ok you think
because the trees will make the blueness
 of the sky blue with the majesty of a waiting king
the grass grows over your face in the glass window
 though there's nowhere to go from here
and the grass will grow over you in a million years
 you cower behind your desk

put on trendy wireless earphones

        and look at the faces in deep concentration around you

it's coffee and brown sugar

        and spreadsheets on your screen

you're waiting for a million years of sleep

        there're ghosts waking up and shuffling

at the corner of your eyes they're raising their hands

        you quickly think of blackbirds on trees far away

and freshwater snails on riverbeds

        where fishes swim around the bend

Greenery

Judy Brown

When I moved to the city that no longer exists
it was September. The air was brown fur
growing thick round the candy cane buildings
that poked through cloud and were lost. I could
breathe, I could talk, but my bones grew longer
and rang when sheet lightning flashed its show
over the mainland. I ate without using knives
or forks – not to be feral, but to slow myself down.
Under the fridge lived one single cockroach
I saw when I ran to the kitchen at midnight for ice.
It was mannerly, seemed not to breed. It knew me.
But I lost myself in the mirrors that covered
one wall of the lounge. I wanted to multiply,
fatten into a crowd. When alone I spoke
of myself as *'we'*. The local clothes suited
me well, and I bought my own air conditioners
to plug the square holes that pierced the walls
of each bedroom. In the evenings I drank and murmured
in the first-person plural, the trees on the hillside
across from the block cooed back from the mirror.
I could hardly see my green self through the trunks.

Laundry

Tara Lee

Apartment blocks stand draped with clothes hanging from every window,
a thousand prayers laundered in workday soap.
Bedsheets must be taken to the roof
where they can billow, fresh as deckle-edged paper,
like sails under high-ceilinged noon.
Waiting out the last days of quarantine in my little hotel room,
I watch the infinite tasks unfold
as unseen hands devote themselves to the ordinary,
attentive to its every crease and wrinkle.
The wakeful handwash cold, no stain too good for care,
while the faithful patiently tend to the self coming and going,
separating, with gentleness, the lights from the darks.
The loving prepare linen for the wedding of each new day,
finding, in the familiar, an unrecognised crispness.
It is the same for everyone.
The life we don't live is the life we pine for,
a wardrobe of pristine, unreal things.

'The neighborhood' by Carmen Lau Ka Man

SIX

'There is a sentence stranded behind this one'

('Translate', Eric Yip)

Introduction to Literature

Huiwen Shi

I ask them to write an essay
on Shirley Jackson's "The Lottery"
and compare it to real life's

victimizing, scapegoating,
mob mentality, human cruelty.

I say exercise close reading
and let your argument lead
the way; textual evidence
shall follow.

Explore, excavate, then explicate.
Find your own voice.

I want them to enjoy freedom
of speech, in this course at least.

But all they want
is a formula that guarantees good grades,
a step-by-step outline to free them
from thinking. They

begin counting the words
of an outstanding essay,
demanding me to stone him

who wrote it, as he failed to follow
the college's sacred tradition
of word limits.

A Pigeon to Deliver a Creole

Lian-Hee Wee

ḢḰ Cántónése ìs dýìng,
īn kēi-sè yòu dìd lót lôẁ.

Many who clammer to save it,

kówtów tò Guángzhôu.
Òr sóme deād péoplé díkssiōnàrỷ
públis̉shdèd īn thè Súng
dié-nāstỳ.
Die more nastily, you mean, like a fetish,
Wòuld reállý bè exemplified by Hóng Kóng Éngēlìsshȅ.
"Thè lánguàge's bōrn a rúnt,"
the teachers grunt.
"Yés-lór, īf yòu sèe-peák éet,
yòur fútúre, nóthìng tò eàt!"
Fínàllỳ àn Ōx àt ā férd
Take up a lah word.
And some poet croon,
às ìf thè fírst tò sée thē moôn.

Pídgìn hátched jǎw, gréw intò crēóle
Or
    is
            it
transfigurated,
From a pigeon tó a croẃ?
"Coc...cold", says the pigeon because
a jaundiced egg laid opposite Peninsula Hotel

— by a downhill turtle who left via Wan Chai —
hatched into a lustrous pearl.
"If we plough like Mui Wo's oxen unrequited,
to re-create our lives in freer pasture,
take with you the speech of the Wick-tóre-whére hábòur,
perhaps
colonizing
    colonized,
is more interwoven than realized.
Coo...cóó...còò"

After Ma Zhiyuan

James Shea

Electric valley, a little wind, indefinite clouds.
An old snail, two monkeys, 6-inch moth on the balcony,
coral-green trees, a bus down the mountain, AC.
Traveler without teeth in the middle of a private street.

譯 / Translate

Eric Yip

Traduttore, traditore
—Italian proverb

If asked to explain 人情味, I'd point to the last cart noodle shop in Kowloon City.

No one knows *placeholder* in Cantonese. At a party, l am Jimmy Carter's interpreter:

this joke is untranslatable, please laugh to save face. There is a sentence stranded

behind this one. I dissolve my tongue in another language. The customs officer

relaxes his scowl. *How is your grandmother?* How I split *grandmother* in two:

嫲嫲, 婆婆—one dead, the other waiting. A life lost in the saying. Dear reader,

sometimes I think you don't know what I mean, if you know what I mean.

Tempo is not a rhythm you sway to

Victoria Fong

You care about me but
you don't know that Tempo
is a tissue paper I use to wipe
my sweat on a hot, humid day
or the rainwater when amber warning hits

I have told you what Tempo is
but you don't need to tell me what Kleenexes are
you want me to tell you all about
牛雜、鴛鴦、渣咋
and maybe I will, after you ask me about
叮叮, star ferries and 小巴
but you'd have go through 有落 yourself

then you'd ask me how I spend my summers
presumably on beaches and on islands
"this summer, last summer,
which summer?" I asked
for summer was never the same
summer changed ever since that day
you would apologise for the question
but there is nothing wrong in asking about summers

*

there is so much we can do
and feel without having to
think about what haunts me
in my lifelong slumber
yet here we are struggling
to put the terrors away

how would I explain what
it means to feel foreign
at home and feel at home
at a foreign place?

Like That

Tom KE Chan

"I didn't expect you to sound like that."
What did you mean *like that*?
Granted, you've never heard me speak,
but you've seen my writing, the way
I use English as my tongue and voice,
the exact same way you use yours.

What did you expect to see?
The foreign chineseness, an Asian
face with squinting eyes, *like that*?
A yellow boy with exotic lisp,
gold-embroidered tunic suit
and set of matching clogs?
A phoenix, a dragon, Bruce Lee? Or
perhaps, the sensual proverb tattooed down my spine:
"When life gives you lemons, drink lemonade."
The way you think it's cool, *like that*?

But then you see me in my clean shirt,
leather jacket and shoes:
the yellow boy with fake hipster look.
You acknowledge the 文青 in me,
a rebel to my own culture.
You greet me with open arms, bow
ninety degrees and breathe
a soft fatherly thrum against my face,
seven decades of good ol' western hospitality,
your British Council accent slowed down just for me.

What is your name? you enunciate.
Yooour naaaame, as the Greensleeves tune
plays on somewhere in the background.

After, I introduced myself in full,
the foreign tongue I mastered to reclaim
my right to be unequivocally heard;
of words, respectfully rephrased
with equal mind and character,
for what should sound and look like Chinese.
If not for myself, I should be glad to be here
for I was chosen by you— the only
featured Hong Kong fiction writer
in your Hong Kong anthology.

As I sat through the lack of Asian representation in the room,
I ponder the possessions that begin in the mind.
Be like water Bruce, and *like that*
I advance, making my way through the cracks.

The Young Biologists

Kate Rogers

They're surprised by the highland city-state,
its valleys' emerald cleavage, swaying
stands of bamboo. In Hong Kong for five days,

Mei-ying and Bogdan joined our hiking group,
hoping for exotic new species.
The swallows stoop low over the dirt trail,

sipping mosquitoes. I stutter to Mei-ying
in rusty Mandarin: *Yenzi lai li.*
She smiles.

Along the shady trail, they spot
a unicorn katydid, a caterpillar blushing
pink like a ripening watermelon.

I list colonial names from my guide,
Hong Kong Butterflies:
Paris Peacock, Chocolate Pansy, Painted Lady.
We shrug and laugh. From a leaf
I scoop a butterfly I do not know, clasp
its torn wings in a loose fist. Glimpse
scattered cells of blue light. The butterfly
tickles my palm.

Striding downhill, my hips grind in sockets
brittle as fossil insects shellacked in sap.
We trade nature tales:

leopard cat—fixing me
in its amber glare while paddling
across a Mai Po *gei wai*.
Mei-ying's sluggish hummingbird
spotted in the barbed
mouth of a Mojave cactus.

Emerging from trees to asphalt path,
we slow. The KCR train clanks
onto the tracks. Trembles the earth.

The blue butterfly flutters
on my palm—lover's eyelashes
against my skin. My new friends
agree it's too ragged to name,
but it can fly. I open my hand.

Brew Sky

Louise Leung Fung Yee

媽媽 invents new vocabs.
Standard English meets 老一輩 when
inflexible tongues pronounce 雞腸 in 錯 geh 讀音。
噒骨 to remove flesh, leaving fundamental structures
with tints of Chinese saliva.

Logo is Local, a symbol to claim
Alphabet colonizes places
There is no "r" in 廣東話——
except for r 痕:
            scratch head when you don't get
            scratch JJ when you horny
            scratch away r-less accent to get 5** in DSE oral
With only 25 alphabets to make names,
"r" finds its place in Hong Konge(r).

Mother's blue sky is brew sky
今晚食乜餸? Housewives shop in wet market 借啲意 to
brag. 小朋友 spills English vocabulary to impress
豬肉佬 and 菜檔姨姨 (but housewives secretly
don't know 啲字點解 too). 天黑 go home 開飯
to only find 字母湯. A soup brewed blood red,
a distance between mother and child under the same sky.

While 媽咪食鹽多過我食米, I eat
alphabet, more than mother.

Gong Nui

Sannya Li

My body is the Gong where you Harbour your fantasies.
Too hungry for your 3PM tea you see her lo4 yau2 eating your bo
    lo yau.
You carefully caress the ripples of cream cones.
Then why wince at my cellulite and tummy rolls?
Go shake the Tai Ping Koon soufflé for some vigorous jiggle!
And maybe adore how my bye-bye arms wiggle?

At cha chaan tengs they ask
  For a *hau5 chit3 jyu1 pa2 faan6.*
On LIHKG a comment says
  "That pork chop thinks she's very jeng"
In *1 Weekly* a headline writes
  BIKINI REVEALS THICK-CUT PORK CHOP THIGHS!

Would writing this make me a Gong Nui?
You know, like, the one who's native in Cantonese
But like writes and speaks in English?
You mock my Honglish accent when I keep my Cantonese intact.
So now I stress the /r/ in Girl.
Then you call me a fake ABC, denying her Hong Kong identity.

My English poems, My English accent –
I'll never be Gong enough for you.
My body, my beauty –
I'll never be Nui enough for you.

*

Yet I'll always write about 港 and code-switch in my lines.
And I'll always poise like 女:
Shoulders broad like the solid 一
Arms crossed like the defiant ㄨ

Gong Nui can be translated to Kong Girl, a slang used to stereotype young Hong Kong women as self-absorbed and whitewashed.
Gong can also be translated to 'harbour' as in Victoria Harbour, a landmark in Hong Kong.
Lo4 yau2 can be translated to 'buttock', which is a pun on the word bo lo yau, a classic Hong Kong pastry.
Hau5 chit3 jyu1 pa2 faan6 can be translated to 'thick-cut pork chop rice', a Hong Kong restaurant classic.
LIHKG is an online discussion forum in Hong Kong.
Pork chop is often used as a metaphor for women with larger body sizes in Hong Kong.
Jeng, when describing the opposite sex, can be translated to 'sexy'.
港 and 女 are the Chinese characters for Gong and Nui respectively.
一 and ㄨ are the brushstrokes of the character 女.

小心

Elizabeth Chung Yi Lei

My little heart does not make me heartless
it makes me careful of who I hand it to.

Her sharp nails
would sooner pierce my soul
than caress my cheek;

His harsh voice
would burst my eardrum,
not sing me to sleep.

Perhaps my little heart
makes me too cautious –
But to never risk a broken heart
is to never be truly loved.

Bak Lan

Madeleine Slavick

I use the Cantonese word for this flower and its tree.

The bus I like to take to the neighbourhood lets me off at a bak lan that stands about eight stories high. We arrive on a slope, mid-tree, enclosed in leaf and scent.

Sometimes at street corners, there are little bags of the flower for sale, a few buds for a few dollars. The person offering is probably over sixty, as is the driver who might place the buds near the dashboard, as if to say to everyone in the vehicle: please be as peaceful as possible.

Several times I have placed a sprig in each of the hands of the people around me, or at their computer keyboard, and once, when a poet died, everyone at the remembrance received the scent. One sprig on each chair.

'White orchid' tells me none of this.

鬼

Wai Julia Cheung

一: My body is a wrapper crinkled in a phone booth, searching for home in a voice, unfolding into a tri-tongued frolic, a dance between language, a language that calls me 鬼妹, its languid sweet bursts of persimmons & wax apples, familiar, but only barely, swinging

words like bodies in a wet market, words that call me鬼妹, fish-flayed & muddied with banter that calls me 鬼妹. *Mother –*

二: Can I claim home knowing only the exterior of a casket? How it opens to let out a steam of bodies teeming thick, like the dim sum basket on my tea table, street bodies roar-torn and trifling with Heaven. Everybody's meat I ration

in my daydreams, laid prostrate in America salivating for return return return. I tell everyone I'm from Hong Kong and they ask 'are you

okay?' Home the name I recognise but a face I dis(re)member. Can I claim its name if I've never seen the bodies? Can I claim (be)longing if the cashier at the Chinese store chooses to speak to me in English? I throat myself into identities and code-switch between selves. I mangle into a me.

三: What is belonging but a longing to be. *Mother, are you there? I'm losing you –*

they call me 鬼 as in ghost and foreigner. Somehow they can all see through me. I cling to my tongue like a possession, and still I am not permitted to own a language. I mispronounce 鬼 into kneel. I swallow my mother-

tongue, static through the wire. I'm here but no bodies home – *can you hear me, mother? They called me American before I've ever been to America.*

First time in America they called me chink.

Fricatives
Eric Yip

To speak English properly, Mrs. Lee said, you must learn
the difference between *three* and *free*. Three men
escaped from Alcatraz in a rubber raft and drowned
on their way to Angel Island. Hear the difference? Try
this: you fought your way into existence. Better. Look
at this picture. Fresh yellow grains beaten
till their seeds spill. That's threshing. That's
submission. You must learn to submit
before you can learn. You must be given
a voice before you can speak. Nobody wants to listen
to a spectacled boy with a Hong Kong accent.
You will have to leave this city, these dark furrows
stuffed full with ancestral bones. Know
that death is thorough. You will speak of bruised bodies
skinnier than yours, force the pen past batons
and blood, call it fresh material for writing. Now they're
paying attention. You're lucky enough
to care how the tongue moves, the seven types
of fricatives, the articulatory function of teeth
sans survival. You will receive a good education
abroad and make your parents proud. You will take
a stranger's cock in your mouth in the piss-slick stall
of that dingy Cantonese restaurant you love and taste
where you came from, what you were made of all along.
Put some work into it, he growls. *C'mon, give me
some bite*. Your mother visits one October, tells you
how everyone speaks differently here, more proper.
You smile, nod, bring her to your favourite restaurant,

order dim sum in English. They're releasing
the students arrested five years ago. *Just a tad more
soy sauce please, thank you.* The television replays
yesterday on repeat. The teapots are refilled. You spoon
served rice into your mouth, this perfect rice.
Steamed, perfect, white.

Permission

Jerrold Yam

Hate to be stereotypical, but how little it takes to
direct attention to ourselves.

First,
willingness.

Selecting a pamphlet-infested alley to brush
shoulders, hold hands,

then doing so. Committing even when the cuff
of my denim jacket

chafes your wrist, pavements pressed thinly against the grey
latticework of shophouses

like a last resort. Long enough for them to step
out from behind the fluorescent

signboards of guesswork: *yup, gei lou, they're together.*
Nod to them, briefly,

then watch sunlight flood corridors
in their eyes.

New Glasses

D.J. Hamilton

—for Kika

So many rainy days, so many
grey clouds tumble over mountaintops
and skyscrapers disappear from sight.

Like the famous falling tree
in the depopulated forest,
does the skyscraper still exist?

Perhaps the better question
when one cannot see the tower
is this, Do I still exist?

How much of the "I" of identity
depends on the "eye" of vision?
Young/old, woman/man, fat/thin

Tall/short, gay/straight, rich/poor,
I am part of all that I have met,
Much have I seen and known; shining cities,

Mountains draped in their fine greenery
climbing up the sides of the sky.
Majestic jungles, and forests filled

with great beasts are part of me,
the sea, when thunderous waves
shake the shore like earthquakes

or sunlight turns to diamonds
on the surface of a tranquil bay
all, are reflected in me. But

can I escape the mirror, the multitudes
of mirrors that are the world?
Can I escape the gaze of others, and

labels hung from chains about my neck
that would mark me, man or woman,
gay or straight, something other than "I"?

Taxicab wipers dance
their never-ending two-step.
Everyone can see it's raining

but today, with new glasses,
I can see the raindrops
each one a little prism, each one

an individual, unique world of its own,
bending light, reflecting all
reflecting my own smiling face

unchained, unlabeled, free.

‘Lost in Stillness. Lost in Flow. 留失。流失。’ by Pui Yan Fong

SEVEN

'"Where Else Should You Be?'
There. Elsewhere.'

('Hoi Polloi', Sam Cheuk)

Home to Hong Kong

Louise Ho

A Chinese
Invited an Irishman
To a Japanese meal
By the Spanish Steps
In the middle of Rome
Having come from Boston
On the way home

Congee in Sham Shui Po

Art Hur

In Sham Shui Po, carefully considering congee.
Carefully considering congee
quietly, completely, in Sham Shui Po.
At night.
Quietly.
I am complete.
I am complete, considerably.
Without the congee,
which I forego completely,
quietly I take my leave
from Sham Shui Po.

Hon Kwong Mansion

Konstandinos Mahoney

I lead him up my road, a narrow skyscraper canyon choked with trapped fumes, turn off into my building, pass a wall of tin mailboxes, climb a flight of stairs to the porter's table - that's him being spoon-fed homemade soup by his mistress. And that cute guy marking a betting card against the wall is from the *Perfect Seafood Restaurant* on the third floor. We squeeze into a lift with a bald monk carrying a water bowl with a white flower floating in it, on his way up to the *Great Perfection Buddhist Centre*, and a buff, tattooed hotty in a tight mesh singlet. He gets off on my floor, disappears into *Bobson's Sauna*, a whiff of sex and steam as the door shuts behind him. We walk on past metal-gates - whoosh of mahjong tiles being washed across a table, someone playing scales on a piano, a TV blaring raucous Cantonese soap. And here we are. Come in, relax, kick off your shoes. Cuddle me.

Demi-Noblesse

Cass Donnelly

There sits by the grimy window in the cha chaan teng
A gentleman in a thin suit and old brogues.
On weekdays he nurses a hot milk tea
And gazes for an hour at silence and smog.
His orders are clipped but exacting;
And his rinsed cutlery placed just so
So one day I slipped in his booth
And he drew himself up and told me this:
"On my way back to my apartment,
the bus stops first behind the building and then in front
If there is some slumbering soul beside me,
I wait for the second stop to rouse them.
So if I do not live lavishly in silk and silver
Or slay suffering before I depart,
Then I will have been a little elegant, a little kind
Even as my city falls apart."

63 Temple Street, Mong Kok

Belle Ling

Remember 63 Temple Street, Mong Kok?
Remember that cha chaan teng,
Mrs Suen, the owner?

Sorry, that jars your ears.
Remember 'leave ice', 'fly sugar leave milk', 'tea go' –
the waiters' breaths, like shooting stars?

Sorry for the monosyllabic dictums.
The imperatives chase me back with their voracious tails
to Mrs Suen's cha chaan teng:
go, leave, fly.

Remember the deep-fried peanut toast –

a square button of butter, egg tassels,
slurry glass eyes of a honey stripe,
and the sweet full-cream condensed milk?

Mrs Suen uses Carnation's
condensed milk
from the contented cows of Australia
– as she says.

As for the peanut butter,
her preference is USA's
Planters' Crunchy, the nuts clutter
but melt like mercy – as she says.

Remember me? Mrs Suen asks.

Remember
the already remembered?
All of us remember –
yet only some grasp the gyration of the remembered.

How can I not remember? Mrs Suen! I reply.

For fifteen years at daybreak the lukewarm TV gargles –
'Welcome to Hong Kong's Morning.'
Every day I eat *deep-fried ghost*, drink *mandarin ducks*, no milk, no sugar.

A diet to keep myself forgotten.

I didn't forget you, Mrs Suen says.
But all of us forget – yet only some let go of the gyration of
the forgotten.

How not to break the fluid egg yolk on my *doll noodles?*
Slightly tilt the egg's fringe up with your chopsticks and pinch –

but the translucent membrane still cracks.
It doesn't forget the way to brokenness, and neither do I.

Grandma sipped the braised pork belly, her last ritual in the hospital.

The rain breaks its back.
It reaches out its little hands
and cut them off in front of me.
It says, *Follow me*. And just as I follow, it vanishes,
and multiplies.

Here's my mobile number, I forgot yours, Mrs Suen says.

Laozi says – 'She forgets it. That's why it lasts forever.'
Did she trade her memory for the eternity of my number?

The rain finds its path to remember,
and falls on every person,

wanting –

> I: One tea set, please.
> Waiter Kuen: Tea set's sold out.
> I: A fast set, then.
> Waiter Kuen: No fast set today.
> I: I'd have a constant set, anyways.
> Waiter Kuen: Constant set is fast set, fast set is tea set.

a fate of return – the rain and Waiter Kuen's back.

Now the rain's a searchlight: a black dog sniffs, a black car follows.
There's no way to see how the rain enters.

You still have much black hair, Mrs Suen, I say.
The rain, stumbling upon its hands, tries to grip a larger surround.

Thanks to the braised pork belly, Mrs Suen jokes.

> *O, O, what a slice!* Grandma exclaimed.
> The fat broke loose on her tongue.
> She never woke up again.

A raindrop is very quiet on my lips.
It melts into a shore afar – to where?

A red bean sneaks out of my glass.
I lick it back – to where?

I forget to give Mrs Suen my mobile number.
The rain has no proper path to rise back as rain.

How does hunger enter me?

I forgot the first bite in my life. I forget why I forgot.

Coolness sprawls flat on my tongue.
I can't even give it a name.

Hoi Polloi

Sam Cheuk

Emulsify, I believe to be the correct
word here; there, elsewhere.
What binds us from the various new
homes is our common language in
food, beadlets of fat surfacing
in congee from the soaked
"oil-fried ghosts."

Once when I was in Paris,
in a Chinese grocery store,
I tried to speak French but didn't,
and the person in an apron tried
to speak English and didn't,
so he spoke Cantonese to me.
Then we talked, wondering perhaps
for a moment how we ended up
here in the quicksilver moment,
how we knew one another
in a language we refuse to forget.

Durs Grunbein, in a poem wrote
about beadlets of fat reflecting
images himself back at him
in a bowl of soup. The oil
in the congee, they look more like
surveillance lenses to me,
interrogating, "Where else
should you be?" There. Elsewhere.

At an East Prussian Restaurant in Berlin

Chris Song

We'd been to a French bar with a neon sign
and tasted spoiled wine and champagne
and drank a toast to old film posters. We left the clatter
of foreign tongues and repaired to a dark street corner
to imagine the sounds of home. We'd seen the underground city
and had peppermint ginger tea under a parasol to suppress fear.
Memory was incised by a church's broken dome
against the sky's gloom. We wondered what was happening
to our home. We looked for an East Prussian restaurant
near Walter-Benjamin-Platz. A family-run ambiance
chased the foreign chill away. The waitress introduced
the etiquette for their traditional dishes. We had a pork knuckle
and a bowl of subdued beetroot soup. Would they
help us understand a country that's been engulfed?
Old posters of town squares, obscure Impressionist paintings
and family pictures hung on the dull yellow walls.
We drank a toast to a wall that's gone thirty years
but heard a picture frame's glass shatter on the floor.
When your home's gone, will the soup go bad?
The din of foreign speech and silverware roused us,
but the leftover wine carried the memory of blood.
Another wall rises anxiously in our hearts.
We buried our faces in the pickle brine of the free world.
There'll be a poetry reading on a square where books had been burned.

Twin Cinema for the Dying Cinema

Hei Yee Hayley Wu

Now showing:
films with
mass appeal
Overpriced popcorn;
feel-good
screenings are
all that
is available.
There is
always
that one
person who
talks too loudly.
Your
gazes glaze over
where ads roll,
and you think
about
stopping for
bubble tea
on
the way out.

streaming means that
live audiences have lost
– rent is theft,
out-of-date for these
at home days.
Best on small-scale screens,
choice
at my fingertips.
No need to
worry about revenue,
obnoxious
attempts to organise staff,
about
'workers' rights'.
When the place
is no more,
if the price is
right there is no
nostalgia. Three stores selling
will fail here. To take
rent, the owners seal
the deal: keeping consumers captive.

It's Late

Janet Charman

it's late in the café on Festival Walk at the back of the Agnes B boutique
the men have coffee and insist on paying for the women's desserts
in the raspberry ice i taste the thin red stripe of your fleecy shirt
is like a pyjama top i once had but on you it fits in that very arresting
XY shape
that goes with the James Dean cut of your leather jacket
which has the zip out inner for when the weather goes below freezing
and this is how it might've looked on JD if he'd been smart enough to
get older
and write novels and scripts and live on The Mainland
and the two of you could be giving up the smokes together
but one time when i was bleeding to death
yes yes bleeding to death
i said to my baby's father 'please stop with the cigarettes'
thinking our children would be half orphans
and he being their sole parent
would need to stick around as long as possible to support their lives
without me
but his reply was: 'i can't'
well
that was that
until fifteen years later just before the cancer he read Allen Carr's
Easyway to Stop Smoking
and quit
but it isn't available in Mandarin although they'd make millions and
millions
out of a translation
i mean here they smoke in the lifts they smoke look i smoked myself
for two
weeks in 1972 and i still inhale on finger cigarettes if i'm driving alone
feeling like shit

Mother's Ink

Kit Fan

somewhere in the pre-history of ink
is reproduction
– Caitríona O'Reilly

Born I was, and wasn't.
She drew breath from the breath she'd lost
to phantom explosions inside her.
Three days, three nights, all breaths
and no food or sleep.

What other mothers had done she did,
re-staging the contractions until my departure.
I saw what she saw:
a cloud of messy flesh waiting at the gate
redder than ink.

The hard plastic on the suction cap.
My misshapen head.
What she remembered I remembered.
A cloudless day at 3 p.m.
and no ink was spilled as she kept herself to herself.

Now and then words escaped from her
bleached hands.
She knew I wanted ink greedily.
She fed it to me, dark milk diluted with water
that, when it touched a page, spread.

She knew it came from the clouds
hiding the teargas and bullets.
She only wanted good ink for me but feared what it meant.
I wanted just ink for her.
I wanted ink more than her.

Sitting in the car with my brother

Jennifer Wong

Watching the worker in front of your car
load and unload boxes.
You stopped by a cafe
so I could get my coffee, the westerner in me
craving what you do not. You told me
you've decided you wouldn't go away:
Not yet. Thinking of your son
who got a place—finally—to your alma mater
you looked up to. *Where the best boys go.*
What we can do is to
love what's still there.
I asked you if you feel
things have changed,
which newspaper should I read.
I'll have to think. & I
find it hard to swallow this
even if you did your best
to steel yourself against it.

Tarrying Home - *Unfolding*

Paola Caronni

At first it seemed that

Nothing could ever compare to you

(what made' you', was yours only)

or to what you were giving in return.

Not even your typhoons

- Fury, wreckage of brambles and branches-

were like the cyclones

sweeping away roofs, cars, homes

in the Northern hemisphere.

It felt familiar,

Always familiar, was

the chattering of parrokets

the call of the koels

covering the irritating rattling of MTR trains

and the horning of taxi drivers unable to unwind.

The trolleys with cardboard boxes pushed by old ladies

The cage homes, the sub-divided flats

everyone wrote about in their Hong Kong poems

were trademarks of your never-changing evolutions.

I liked to fall asleep listening to your loud lullaby

I liked to stay with you despite the hype, the high price;

I thought it was almost forever-love

despite the smog, the smoke, the snakes, the blaze.

Then, when the trees,

When even the banyans changed shape and turned into bamboos,

when they started bending at the slightest whisper of wind,

that love burned to ashes,

like the joss-paper everyone wrote about

in their Hong Kong poems.

You entered another door,

This time...

Me, following you,

hopeful at first—

circling around like a koi prisoner in the pond,

heart in my hands

looking for the exit in the dark hall

ready to leave you forever.

Again

Felix Chow Yue Ching

Goodbye, in Cantonese, is usually a promise.
再見. See you again.
The words climbed out of me
like they were leaving a country
and severed my tongue on the way.

We tell each other that *everyone's moving*
ignoring Facebook stories
of fingers worn to the bone,
visas forming the whetstone.

Delight dies in departure halls. We are just
another 死黨 and 巴打
another lover and lover
another ma ma and granddaughter
making the most of our hugs, believing

there is no cure for a rotting city
seeping through redaction and inaction
torn apart by the times.

再見, if we can. Through Zoom or Plexiglass.
We promise to visit
and match our annual leave,
teach your kid Cantonese.
We are both kidding ourselves.

I watch you walk through the gateway
beyond the claw-end of the dragon
and put, behind,
a sun-bitten harbour
rusting with colour.

Gratitude on Ch'in's Edge
Marilyn Chin

Let grief convert to anger, blunt not the heart

For M.O.

Lotus: white silent fist flower

Unfurling on Buddha's palm

Truth shall erupt any moment now

Mrs. Wong grows silk flowers they don't wilt or die

Plastic ones are ugly to a trained girl's eye

*

Most beautiful girl, don't grow old, don't die

Don't rot in the vase while others thrive

They cut you, then wrap you in a plastic shroud

Scatter your yellow ashes to offend the cosmos

They lionize you, malathion you

Your thorns are cherished by Morticia's clippers

Valentine's Day, birthdays, a garland for caskets

Piss a brief scent then sweeten the garbage

*

Oh, wretched one, your breath is sour this morning

I'll brew a cup of joe for you and kiss your forehead

Turn up the Manilow to lighten your sick bed

No need to speak now, the respirator won't save you

*

The bastard slumped in the chair is the ghost of the emperor

He orders your mother around in the abandoned palace

Even in death, mother, you cannot shut his pie hole

He spits out rice because the kernels are too hard

Flesh too raw   cabbage too bland   no hot food   on cold food day

Let's poison his pablum   rescue the maiden

Crawl into his leather skin   and change destiny

*

Control me, I'm mad, I'm low on meds

They torture my mind with sonnets about ranunculus

Whitman had a beautiful cock   Emily was more god than love

I'm slurping frog noodles   at an ancient frog pond

I'll teach them proper English like a proper Chinaman

*

Twenty years in this institution and I finally see light

My eyes once shuttered   by whiteboard obedience

I cleaned out my desk   they crossed out my eyes

The pupils circling inward   in search of renaissance

*

I am grateful for Gogol's freaking coat

Made of pleather and New Zealand lambskin

Some wise ass Chinese girl sewed it   in the economic miracle zone

Some jackass stole it from me   while I was teaching "forms"

Dumped into the garbage bin   marked "recyclable"

*

Let me peel off my skin for you   tanned with eternity's blood

Pocked by uncertainty   walking downcast in sun

California is seasonless   but the sun will burn you senseless

A good place to read "The Banality of Evil"

*

Thank you very much   thank you very much

For my green card   for my freedom

For my second   and third dose

Of comeuppance

But Pikachu says

F U very much   F U you very much

Something got lost in translation

*

Rap and sing nephews, dream big, love hard

Sisters, play the lyre and birth rosy children

Become Vice President   of merchandizing   own the store!

Ride the gravy train of light

Be realistic with a tinge of margin

Sometimes the bear eats you   sometimes he eats your

Quince

*

Love the Leviathan   pinch him   make him feel grace

Paint a lovely sunset   slap him on the head

Take off your robe and say   the scars have not healed

If that doesn't work   just walk away from THE MAN

*

The five colors of the sunset make me blind

The five sounds of lyre make me deaf

The five tastes make me lose my sense of taste

How long have you been exiled, Li Bai?

Tu Fu, why did they send you to the outpost?

I come naked   I leave naked

But give me back   my soul!

*

Bow down in submission   and you will be preserved

Be bottom   be motionless   a low-lying delta

Let the predators   think you are dead

Let them plow the wetlands   erect their subdivisions

Let them plant their flag   and dream of the West Indies

*

Beg at the door of eternity   you arrogant Airedale

Scoop the senseless kitty litter   without shame

Who is your nemesis, Dr. Moriarty?   A spy in the poetry academy?

The ailing autarky   of sabotage

And pain

*

Wrestle with Laozi   while listening to Bitch's Brew

Blow my head off says Emily   kill me softly covers Lauryn

The space between life and death   is a faint aroma of sadness

The border is closing   at Peach Blossom Spring

*

I bow and bow and say thank you very much

I bow and bow and say love your sister

I bow and bow and say thank you very much

I bow and bow and say forgive your father

I bow and bow and say thank you very much

I bow and bow and say let your freak flags fly

I bow and bow to some   motherless   headless god

*

A low-lying valley am I, old dude, a low-lying valley

Let the white troops ride over   waving tiny red flags

Let the red guards follow   waving tiny white flags

I feel so alone   so alone   so alone

Trapped between the R train   and Voldemort

*

I bow and bow to a waning horizon

I bow and bow to ventilator mist

I bow and bow to blue quietude

I bow and bow to twitter piss

I bow and bow to the night blooming cereus

I bow and bow to her fragile green nape

I bow and bow to the flash of the sickle

I bow to the head of Marie Antoinette

*

Girl poet: all lifelong you honoured perfection

But the schoolyard   is foul   lunatic   depraved

They will slay you for being 'the heathen chinee!'

For being 'the perpetual foreigner!'

*

Thank you   Uncle Zhuangzi   for your diaphanous nightgown

Thank you   Auntie Phillis   for your clarion black dress

Butterfly   fluttering her fake eyelashes

West of Ch'in's edge   is our caravan   of lost dreams

想(家)

Hilary Tam

in the airport bathroom, you watch your reflection sink
in the stopper, faulty fluorescent lights flickering in your mouth.
the soap suds wash you clean, glowing. a fresh
start. once, you started to cry on the taxi ride home,
the driver silent and staring through the hanging lotus tassels.
Even without looking, you knew each hue and hum of the cityscape.
you knew how easily in your dreams their shadows would blaze
as a technicolor ghost town. maybe it will all stay the same,
really. the midtown highways will snake just as they do.
阿媽 will peel her nightly oranges at the same table
that you stained with coffee, the quiet language of love
still pithy and sweet. once, you held hands with 阿爸
at the street market and wondered how it would feel
to let go. now you repeat his cantonese slang, fogging up
the mirror cabinet, words already chopped on a treacherous
tongue. you wonder when you will forget the euphemisms
for leaving, for regret. 阿爸阿媽 are waiting outside
on the cold boarding gate benches. they are smiling,
telling each other about the time a little girl
sat on their shoulders, wide-eyed, and shrieked
at the world below. you want to say, *she is still here.*

'Untitled' by Tung Pang Lam

ACKNOWLEDGEMENTS

The poems in this anthology are reprinted from the following books, journals, magazines, anthologies, and online platforms, all by permission of the publishers listed unless stated otherwise. Thanks are due to all the copyright holders cited below for their kind permission:

Martin Alexander's poem 'Hoi Ha' first appeared in *Clearing Ground* (Chameleon Press, 2004).

Gillian Barbara Bickley's poem 'Change with Constancy' first appeared in *Moving House and Other Poems from Hong Kong* (Proverse Hong Kong, 2005).

Robert Black's poem 'Two Candles (婉)' first appeared in *Ocean Pound's Monday Art Post* (June 2015).

Helen Bowell's poem 'Yung Shue Wan Pier' first appeared in *The Willowherb Review*, Issue 3 (2020).

Judy Brown's poem 'Greenery' first appeared in *Lairs* (Seren, 2022) and National Poetry Day website.

Dorothy Chan's poem 'Triple Sonnet for Veronica Lodge's Tigers' first appeared in *HAD* (2021).

Jessica Chan's poem 'Madame X' first appeared in *Voice & Verse Poetry Magazine*, Issue 43 (2018).

Mary Jean Chan's poem 'Calling Home' first appeared in *The Poetry Review*, Issue 111.1 (2021).

Stephanie Chang's poem 'Lotus Flower Kingdom' first appeared in *The Adroit Journal*, Issue 39 (2021).

Janet Charman's poem 'It's late' first appeared in 仁 *surrender* (Otago University Press, 2017).

Tim Tim Cheng's poem 'Self-Portrait of My Granny in the Voice of Anti-Japanese Drama's Protagonist' first appeared in *Tapping at Glass*

(VERVE Poetry Press, 2023).

Marilyn Chin's poem 'Gratitude on Ch'in's Edge' will be featured in Chin's forthcoming book *SAGE* (W.W. Norton, 2023).

Felix Chow Yue Ching's poem '英年早逝' first appeared in *IDEAS JOURNAL* (2022).

Claire Cox's poem 'Eye' first appeared in *The Poetry School 'Poems' Blog.*

River 瑩瑩 Dandelion's poem 'How We Survived: 爺爺's Pantoum (II)' first appeared in *Shade Literary Arts,* Fall/Winter Issue (2021).

Cecil Calsas Elleran's poem 'Checherella' first appeared in *Wishing Well: Voices from Foreign Domestic Workers in Hong Kong and Beyond* (2016).

Nashua Gallagher's poem 'Siu Ap Fan with a Visitor' first appeared in *All The Words a Stage* (Chameleon Press, 2018).

Louise Ho's poems 'Island' and 'Home to Hong Kong' first appeared in *New Beginnings, Old Ends* (Asia 2000 Ltd, 1997).

Viki Holmes's poem 'Border Town' first appeared in *Girls' Adventure Stories of Long Ago* (Chameleon Press, 2018).

Sarah Howe's poem 'Calendar' first appeared in *MUSEA - A book of modern muses* (Condé Nast, 2019).

Akin Jeje's poem 'Ping Shan Heritage Trail' first appeared in *Smoked Pearl: Poems of Hong Kong and Beyond* (Proverse Hong Kong, 2010).

Kavita A. Jindal's poem 'Dealing in Numbers' first appeared in *Stand,* Volume 15 (2017).

Sannya Li's poem 'Gong Nui' first appeared in *Cha: An Asian Literary Journal (The Auditory Cortex Edition).*

Belle Ling's poem '63 Temple Street, Mong Kok' first appeared in *Australian Book Review,* Volume 409 (2019).

David McKirdy's poem 'Citizen Ship' and 'Star Struck' first appeared in *Ancestral Worship* (Chameleon Press, 2014).

Collier Nogues's poem 'There is a Season Waiting Behind This One' first appeared in *Cha: An Asian Literary Journal* (2020).

Mani Rao's poem 'The Dotted Line' first appeared in *Usawa Literary Review*, Issue 7 (2022).

Harry Ricketts's poem 'Repulse Bay Hotel, Hong Kong' first appeared in *Your Secret Life* (HeadworX, 2005).

James Shea's poems 'Soft Tank' first appeared in *Fleur des Lettres, Special Issue* (September 2014) and 'After Ma Zhiyuan' first appeared in *North American Review*, Volume 301, no. 4 (2016).

Huiwen Shi's poem 'Introduction to Literature' first appeared in 2rulesofwriting.com (6 April 2022).

Madeleine Slavick 思樂維's poem 'Bak Lan' first appeared in *Fifty Stories Fifty Images* (MCCM Creations, 2012).

Chris Song's poem 'At an East Prussian Restaurant in Berlin' first appeared in *Voice & Verse Poetry Magazine*, Issue 69 (2023).

Jennifer Lee Tsai's poem 'Kuk Po' first appeared in *Wild Court* (13 October 2020).

Mags Webster's poem 'Different Skin' first appeared in *Nothing to Declare* (Puncher and Wattmann, 2020) and *Halfway Home* (City University of Hong Kong, 2014).

Lian-Hee Wee's poem 'A Pigeon to Deliver a Creole' first appeared on the *Kongpowrimo* Facebook page (2022).

Jane Wong's poem 'Special Economic Zone Love Song' first appeared in *Dusie*, Issue 19 (2016).

Hei Yee Hayley Wu's poem 'Twin Cinema for the Dying Cinema' first appeared in *The Liminal Review*, Issue 1 (2021).

Eric Yip's poem '譯 / Translate' first appeared in *harana poetry*, Issue 10 (2022) and 'Fricatives' was published in *Poetry Review*, Issue 112.1 (2022).

Our thanks to the following people and institutions who have offered support to this anthology project: Leeds Centre for New Chinese Writing (https://writingchinese.leeds.ac.uk/), *Stand* magazine (https://www.standmagazine.org/), Ben Kwok, William Chu, Luke Au, Karen Kong, Juan José Morales, Connie Yau, Sandy Wong, Tse's Noodles Oxford, and an anonymous donor 'who would love to make Hong Kong poets more known and visible to the whole world'.

'Outside Golden Elderly Restaurant' by Kayla Lui

THE POETS & ARTISTS

Martin Alexander is an award-winning poet and writer whose work has been widely published. He has won the RTHK-SCMP short story competition and Romania's Orient-Occident International Grand Prix for Poetry. A featured author at literary festivals worldwide, he was for some years a trustee of the UK's Poetry Society and Editor in Chief of the *Asia Literary Review*. Alexander has also edited a number of books, most recently Audrey Donnithorne's *China in Life's Foreground* (Australian Scholarly Publishing, 2019).

Wahyan Au is a Hong Kong based artist and a printmaker whose drawings and illustrations have been published in numerous local magazines and newspapers, including her comic strip *Me1 World* in Sunday Mingpao. She has devoted much of her creative efforts to print-making and self-publishing in recent years. A collection of short stories in print *Dreams of a Toad* was published in 2019 and her first short comic *Praying Mantis Combat* was published a year after. Sometimes she writes, sometimes she draws.

John Wall Barger's poems and critical writing have appeared in *American Poetry Review, Kenyon Review, Poetry Ireland Review,* and *Best of the Best Canadian Poetry.* His sixth book, *Smog Mother* (Palimpsest Press), came out in fall 2022. He is a contract editor for *Frontenac House,* and teaches Creative Writing at The University of the Arts in Philadelphia.

Andrew Barker has lived in Hong Kong since 1996. He is a literature professor and the operator of the poetry lectures website Mycroftlectures.com where readings of his poetry can be found. He has published the collections *Snowblind from my Protective Colouring, Joyce is Not Here: 101 Modern Shakespearean Sonnets* and *Orange Peel: Modern Shakespearean Sonnets Book 2. Sonnets 102-203* which are available on Amazon, and is currently completing *Social Room: Modern Shakespearean Sonnets Book 3. Sonnets 204-305.*

Gillian Bickley was born and educated in the UK and has lived mainly in Hong Kong since 1970, primarily as an academic, but also as a subject officer for the then Hong Kong Examinations Authority, an editor with the then Longman Far East (now Pearson) and now a publisher and literary prize founder/administrator. Some of her seven poetry collections received publication support from the Hong Kong Arts

Development Council. She also researches and publishes in the area of nineteenth-century Hong Kong.

Robert Black is an award-winning poet and photographer currently based in Toronto. Born in California, he lived part of his childhood in Taipei, Taiwan and Hong Kong before returning to the U.S. He has published his poems, essays and short fiction in magazines and journals in the US, Canada, Australia, Russia, France, Japan, Taiwan and Hong Kong. He has exhibited his photographs in group and solo shows in Canada, Japan, Russia, Australia, France, Hong Kong, Taiwan and the US and has been included in a number of photography publications. He currently resides in Toronto. His book of poetry *Voyage Voyager, Ghosts* is forthcoming.

Helen Bowell is a poet, editor, producer and facilitator. She is a co-director of Dead [Women] Poets Society and runs the Bi+ Lines project, editing the first anthology of bi+ poets in English. She is a Ledbury Poetry Critic and her debut pamphlet *The Barman* (Bad Betty Press, 2022) was a Poetry Book Society Pamphlet Choice.

Judy Brown's third collection is *Lairs* (Seren 2022). Her earlier books, both published by Seren, were *Loudness* (2011), shortlisted for the Forward and Aldeburgh prizes for best first collection, and *Crowd Sensations* (2016), shortlisted for the Ledbury Forte Prize. Judy was Poet-in-Residence at the Wordsworth Trust during 2013, before which she worked as a lawyer in London and Hong Kong.

Paola Caronni was born in Italy and has been living in Asia for over twenty years. Paola holds an MFA in Creative Writing from the University of Hong Kong. Her poems have been published or are forthcoming in various printed anthologies and online literary journals (*American Writers Review, Voice & Verse Poetry Magazine; The Curator; Cha: An Asian Literary Journal; The Wild Word; New Asian Writing; Wisconsin Review; From Whispers to Roars,* and others). Paola's first poetry collection *Uncharted Waters* (2021) received a Hong Kong Arts Development Council grant and won the Proverse Prize in 2020.

Dorothy Chan is the author of five poetry collections, including the forthcoming, *Return of the Chinese Femme* (Deep Vellum Books Fall 2023 / Spring 2024). They are an Assistant Professor of English at the

University of Wisconsin-Eau Claire and Co-Founder and Editor-in-Chief of *Honey Literary Inc*, 501(c)(3) BIPOC literary arts organisation, run by women, femme, and queer editors of colour.

Janet Bi Li Chan is a poet, artist and scholar born in Hong Kong. She left Hong Kong in 1965, studied and worked in Canada for many years and now lives in Australia. She has numerous scholarly publications as a sociologist and is currently Emeritus Professor at UNSW Sydney. Her artwork has been shown in both group and solo exhibitions. Her poetry has been published in a multi-media exhibition 'Soft Power', in *Visual Verse, The Poet, the Moon Orchard Audiobook,* and *Under the Radar*. Her poetry collection was short-listed for publication by Liquid Amber Press for 2023.

Jessica Chan is a writer of poems and short stories. Her work has appeared or is forthcoming in *Voice & Verse Poetry Magazine, Proverse Prize Anthology 2020, opia* and others. She is a recipient of a Hong Kong Top Story Award in 2012 and 2014 and has been recognised in the Tower Poetry competition. She recently finished a MSt in Creative Writing at the University of Cambridge and can be found lurking in Hong Kong. Find her on twitter @awildjesswrites.

Mary Jean Chan is the author of two poetry collections: *Flèche* (Faber, 2019) and *Bright Fear* (Faber, 2023). They co-edited the anthology *100 Queer Poems* (Vintage, 2022) with Andrew McMillan. Chan is a judge for the 2023 Booker Prize, and currently serves as Senior Lecturer in Creative Writing (Poetry) at Oxford Brookes University.

Tom K.E. Chan holds an MFA at the University of Hong Kong, where he also holds his BA in Language and Communication. He is a poet for OutLoud HK and Peel Street Poetry. His poetry chapbook is published in *Earthbound Press Poetry Series* (Vo.2, No.7). His other poems are published in *Proverse Hong Kong, HKVanities, Cha: An Asian Literary Journal* and *Voice & Verse Poetry Magazine*. His short story, 'The Battle of the Masks', was published in the Hong Kong Writers Circle's 17th Anthology, *After the Storm*.

Yvette Chan is a poet, screenwriter, and storyboard artist from Hong Kong. She strives to experiment with the boundaries of art, often combining visual and aural elements when presenting her written pieces. She is a First Class graduate of the University of Warwick in English Literature and Creative Writing and was head editor of their literary and arts magazine *Kamena*. Her poetry has been published by the *borderline, celestite poetry, Tigers Zine* with more publications awaiting. Her poem 'One Year Older' was shortlisted by Wells Festival of Literature, Young Poets' Competition 2021.

Stephanie Chang (she/they) is an undergraduate student at Kenyon College, where she received the $60,000 S. Georgia Nugent Award in Creative Writing. Her work appears or is forthcoming in *The Rumpus, Adroit Journal, Offing, Strange Horizons, Waxwing, Penn Review*, and others. She studies Art History, Sociology, and English. Currently, she serves as the Editor-in-Chief of *The OROTONE Journal*.

Janet Charman's latest collection is The Pistils (OUP 2022). Her collection 仁 *Surrender* (OUP 2017) chronicles her writing residencies in Hong Kong and Taiwan. Her essay, 'Allen Curnow's suppression of the poetics of Mary Stanley', appeared in *Women's Studies Journal*, Volume 33 Number 1/2, December 2019: 103-112. A monograph *Smoking: The Homoerotic Subtext of 'Man Alone' - A Matrixial Reading*, Genrebooks, (Dunedin, 2018), is free to download at: http://www.genrebooks.co.nz. Janet Charman won the 2008 Montana Book Award for Poetry for her sixth collection *Cold Snack* (AUP 2007).

Sam Cheuk is a Hong Kong-born Canadian author of *Love Figures, Deus et Machina*, and *Postscripts from a City Burning*. He is currently working on *Marginalia*, which examines the function, execution, and generative potential behind censorship. Cheuk lives in Vancouver.

Atom Cheung writes from home in beautiful Shek Kip Mei. His latest poetry and prose can be found in *Canto Cutie, The Dillydoun Review*, and *LickZine*. He also publishes zines and hybrid works under the name Atom Alicia C. He is a radio presenter on RTHK and keeps an experimental audio blog via the podcast Atomic Heart. More at www.atomcheung.com.

Wai Julia Cheung is a poet from Hong Kong, currently living in Boston, contemplating the transactional absurdity and alienation in our day to day living. Perpetually in conflict with herself, she struggles with the distances between the voices she embodies – e.g. working in both corporate and corporage, she's in the process of figuring out what corpo-real is. You will likely find her overthinking, or on her twitter, @creaturewai.

Marilyn Chin is an award-winning poet and her works have become Asian American classics and are taught all over the world. She is an author of six books of poems and a book of fiction. Her most recent books are *Sage* and *A Portrait of the Self as Nation: New and Selected Poems*. She has won numerous awards, including the Ruth Lilly Prize, the Anisfield Wolf Book Award, the United States Artist Foundation Award, the Radcliffe Institute Fellowship at Harvard, the Rockefeller, two National Endowment for the Arts Awards and others. She is featured in major anthologies, including *The Penguin Anthology of 20th Century American Poetry*. She serves as Professor Emerita of San Diego State University and as a Chancellor of the Academy of American Poets.

Felix Chow Yue Ching is a MPhil student at the University of Hong Kong. He double-majored in English Studies and Hong Kong Studies at HKU, achieving first-class honours. He is the winner of the The HKBU Century Club Citywide English Poetry Competition, The Maisie Choa English Poetry Prize, The Joseph Yau Sai Man Memorial Prize in English Literature and The Yuet Hing and Ho Sin Ming Prize in Hong Kong Studies. His poems are published in *The Lincoln Review*, *Voice & Verse Poetry Magazine* and *Cha: Asian Literary Journal*. He is a co-organiser of OutLoud HK, Hong Kong's longest-running English poetry collective. Forever a HongKonger.

Elizabeth Chung Yi Lei, or **Lilli**, completed her undergraduate degree in English Literature and Theatre Studies (International) at the University of Leeds, an exchange year at the University of Hong Kong, and her MPhil in English (Literary Studies) at the Chinese University of Hong Kong (CUHK), focussing on Hong Kong Literature and Space-Place Theory. She recently began her PhD studies at CUHK, where she intends to continue her research with a focus on temporality and expression.

Born in Hong Kong, **Claire Cox** now lives and works in Oxfordshire. She is co-founder and Associate Editor at ignition press, a publisher which won 2021 Michael Marks Publishers' Award, and has completed her practice-based PhD at Royal Holloway, University of London, studying poetry and disaster. She was one of three winning poets included in *Primers: Volume Five* (Nine Arches Press, 2020) and the winner of the 2020 Wigtown Alastair Reid Pamphlet Prize.

River 瑩瑩 Dandelion, formerly known as huiying, is a keeper of ancestral medicine through writing poetry, teaching, and creating ceremony. He writes to connect with the unseen so we can feel and heal. River's work is published in *Best New Poets, The Offing, Asian American Journal of Psychology,* and elsewhere. A recipient of fellowships from Tin House and Kundiman, River has also travelled to Chinatowns around the world to document stories of diaspora. For more: riverdandelion.com.

Cass Donnelly exists. She is a writing enthusiast who dabbles in prose and poetry, and currently has no published works anywhere.

Cecil C. Elleran has savoured the scent of the fragrant harbour since 2007 and 15 years later is an ethnic minority writer representing migrant worker issues through prose and poetry. Some of her works have been published online and in print. She performed on TEDxWanChai back in June 2018 and has spoken to anthropology students at Chinese University of Hong Kong. She goes to Peel Street Poetry regularly and considers Hong Kong as her second home.

Kit Fan's third poetry collection *The Ink Cloud Reader* was published by Carcanet in April 2023. He is the author of two other books of poems, *As Slow As Possible* (2018) and *Paper Scissors Stone* (2011). His debut novel is *Diamond Hill* (2021). He was elected a Fellow of the Royal Society of Literature in 2022.

Pui Yan Fong is a visual arts artist who was born in Hong Kong and raised in Macau. Since 2017, she has lived in Germany to pursue her higher education and is currently doing an MA in Cultural Studies at Leuphana University. Through illustrations and sculptures accompanied by writings, she explores the complex relations between her experiences on migration, language, identity and the haunting question of what makes a home, home.

Victoria Fong, born and raised in Hong Kong, majored in Global Communication at the Chinese University of Hong Kong. They have a fondness for the city and hope that Hong Kong's literary scene would gain more appreciation and recognition.

Nashua Gallagher is the Sri-Lankan born, Hong Kong-raised author of *All the Words a Stage* (Chameleon Press, 2018). She is the founding director of Peel Street Poetry, a literary collective in Hong Kong. Her work sits somewhere between page and stage and has been anthologised widely across different mediums. She currently lives in Zurich.

D.J. Hamilton's recent book of poems, *The Hummingbird Sometimes Flies Backwards,* won the Proverse Prize. He has won awards in Washington State and New York for poems, plays and play directing. His poems have appeared in *Ofi Press, Repentino, Dalmoma, Firecrackers, Bumbershoot Anthology, Compages,* and other publications. Hamilton grew up in Wisconsin and later lived in Seattle and in Port Townsend, Washington, where the writers and editors of Empty Bowl and Copper Canyon Press became friends and mentors. After 28 years in Washington State, 11 years in Mexico and 8 in Asia, he sees himself as a US- Mexico-Hong Kong writer. He lives in Hong Kong.

Louise Ho is one of Hong Kong's most recognised contemporary poets writing in English. Born and brought up mostly in Hong Kong, she has lived in Mauritius, England, America and Australia. She was Associate Professor of English at the Chinese University of Hong Kong, where she taught English and American poetry, Shakespeare and, briefly, creative writing. She has four collections of poetry: *Sheung Shui Pastoral; Local Habitation; New Ends, Old Beginnings;* and *Incense Trees*. Ho is retired and now lives and writes in Australia and Hong Kong.

Polly Ho Sai Fung graduated from the University of Hong Kong. She has been devoting her time organising poetry readings at Kubrick Poetry since 2007. She started KPS (Kubrick Poetry Society), an online writing school to nurture and facilitate poetry writing and fiction writing during the outbreak of covid in 2020.

Tammy Lai-Ming Ho is the Editor-in-Chief of *Cha: An Asian Literary Journal*, the English Editor of *Voice & Verse Poetry Magazine*, and co-editor of the academic journal *Hong Kong Studies*.

Henrik Hoeg is a Danish poet living in Hong Kong, where he runs Hong

Kong's largest open mic Peel Street Poetry. He has published three collections of poetry, the most recent of which is *Birth is the Coward's Way In* from Trivial Disaster Publishing. His bio contains exactly fifty-two words. Exactly.

Viki Holmes is a widely anthologised and prize-winning British poet and performer who began her writing career in Cardiff as part of the Happy Demon poetry collective. Her poetry has appeared in literary magazines and anthologies in Wales, England, Hong Kong, Australia, Canada, Macao and Singapore. She was twice a finalist in the John Tripp Award for Spoken Poetry (Wales), and was a runner-up in Hong Kong's inaugural Poetry Slam. Her first collection, *miss moon's class*, is published by Chameleon Press (Hong Kong) and she is co-editor of the Haven (Hong Kong) anthology of world women's writing *Not A Muse*. She currently lives and works in Japan.

Sarah Howe is a Hong Kong-born poet, academic and editor, and now lives in London. Her first book *Loop of Jade* (Chatto & Windus, 2015) won the T.S. Eliot Prize and The Sunday Times / PFD Young Writer of the Year Award. She teaches poetry at King's College London.

May Huang 黃鴻霙 is a writer and translator from Hong Kong and Taiwan. Her work has appeared in *Electric Literature, Words Without Borders, World Literature Today, The Commons,* and elsewhere. She is a PEN/HEIM grant recipient and former ALTA Emerging Translator. Her translation of Derek Chung's *A Cha Chaan Teng That Does Not Exist* is forthcoming from Zephyr Press in 2023. Based in Berkeley, she works in public relations and enjoys constructing crosswords. Twitter: @mayhuangwrites

Antony Huen has published poems in *The Dark Horse, Poetry Wales, PN Review,* and others. As a critic, he won the inaugural *Wasafiri* Essay Prize and the silver medal for the inaugural essay prize of *Women: A Cultural Review*. He holds an MA in Creative Writing from Birmingham and a PhD in English from York.

Ian Humphreys's debut collection *Zebra* (Nine Arches Press) was nominated for the Portico Prize. His second collection *Tormentil* (Nine Arches, 2023) won a Royal Society of Literature 'Literature Matters' Award while in progress. Ian is the editor of *Why I Write Poetry* (Nine

Arches), and the producer and co-editor of *After Sylvia: Poems and Essays in Celebration of Sylvia Plath* (Nine Arches). Ian is widely published in journals, including *The Poetry Review, The Rialto* and *Poetry London*, and has written for the BBC.

Art Hur is a writer and painter whose work focuses on language, dealing with social anxiety, and healing from trauma. He lives in Hong Kong.

Canadian poet **Akin Jeje** lives in Hong Kong. Jeje's works have been featured in Canada, the United States, Singapore and Hong Kong. His first collection *Smoked Pearl* was longlisted for the 2009 International Proverse Prize and published in 2010. Jeje's most recent publication, 'Too Long' is in Hong Kong's *Voice & Verse Poetry Magazine*. He is currently at work on another full-length poetry collection tentatively entitled *write about here*. Jeje is also a regular contributor to *Cha: An Asian Literary Journal*.

Kavita A. Jindal is the author of *Manual For A Decent Life* which won the Eastern Eye Award for Literature, 2020. Her poetry books are *Raincheck Accepted, Raincheck Renewed* and *Patina*. Her work has appeared in anthologies and journals worldwide and been broadcast on BBC Radio, Zee TV and European radio stations. She served as Senior Editor at *Asia Literary Review* and is co-founder of The Whole Kahani writers' collective. Kavita lived and worked in Hong Kong for thirteen years.

Peter Kennedy holds degrees from the universities of Bristol, Sussex, Wales, Essex and Trinity College Dublin. He has taught in England, Greece, Czechoslovakia, Romania, Saudi Arabia, China, Brunei and, since 1988, in Hong Kong (Associate Professor at SPACE, HKU). He is Honorary Associate Professor, since 2013, in the School of English, HKU where he teaches B.A. courses on poetry and on James Joyce. His five books and his journal articles have been mainly concerned with adult learning and learning English through literature. He has also published a volume of verse.

Sean Wai Keung is a Glasgow-based performance maker and writer whose work often explores concepts of mixed-ness, identity and migration. His first full length poetry collection *sikfan glaschu* was published by VERVE Poetry Press in April 2021 and subsequently shortlisted for the 2022 Kavya Prize. He has worked with organisations including the Scottish BPOC Writers Network, the National Theatre of Scotland and *Gutter Magazine*, to name a few. For more information, please visit seanwaikeung.carrd.co

Agnes S. L. Lam, an Honorary Fellow in Writing by the University of Iowa (2008), has published *Woman to Woman and Other Poems* (1997), Water Wood Pure Splendour (2001), *A Pond in the Sky* (2013), *Poppies by the Motorway* (2017) and *Becoming Poets: The Asian English Experience* (2014).

Tung Pang Lam 林東鵬 lives and works in North America and Hong Kong. His artistic practice encompasses painting, drawing, performance, video, and installation. Assembling traditional iconography and found objects, Lam creates layered allegorical landscapes that engage themes of history, memory, and time. He engages the themes of collective memories and fleeting nostalgia, which articulate an ongoing negotiation of the overlapping city-state's reality. In his allegorical landscapes, journeys and sceneries become essential passages connecting time and distance, longing and loss.

Carmen Lau Ka Man graduated from Lingnan University with a degree in Visual Studies in 2021. Painting is her primary medium, with most of her works drawn from life. Lau is interested in exploring the relationship between art and self, tracing back to her personal growth, trauma, and daily experience.

Sophie Lau is a freelance writer and educator (and generally vibing polyglot!) of Hakka heritage based in the UK. She writes various non-fiction bits and bobs and is currently working on a book that centres on life in Hong Kong, for which she recently completed a residency with Bothy Project. Sophie also facilitates workshops in and outwith schools alongside her work as a languages tutor. In her free time, she enjoys hanging out with her dogs, Doughnut and Tiny, and solo-travelling with her film camera in hand!

Wendelin Law (@wendylawwrites) is a poet and writer who grew up in Tuen Mun. She can confirm that people in Tuen Mun do not travel by riding on cows. She loves egg tarts (shortcrust instead of puff pastry) and vitasoy milk (oat). But what she loves most about Hong Kong, apart from food, MK culture and Cantopop, is the resilience of its people. She is the winner of the VERVE Poetry Festival Competition 2023 judged by Kim Moore, and was shortlisted in the Magma Poetry Pamphlet Competition 2022.

Laura Jane Lee is a Hong Kong-born, Singapore-based poet. She founded KongPoWriMo, and is a winner of the Sir Roger Newdigate Prize and various international poetry competitions. Her work has been featured in *The Straits Times, Tatler Asia, Poetry London, Ambit, QLRS,* and the 52nd Poetry International Festival in Rotterdam. Laura Jane is also the Poetry Editor of *SPLOOSH Magazine*, and has published pamphlets *chengyu: chinoiserie* and *flinch & air*.

Swann Adara Lee (hir/zie) is a Hong Kong-based writer and undergraduate of mixed Southeast Asian descent. Hir works focus mainly on inner plurality, bodies of water, and posthumanism - having been featured in *Humana Obscura, Daisyworld Magazine,* and *Life on Lantau*. Aside from writing, zie enjoys bugwatching on his native Lantau Island and slowly building a suit of armour out of discarded beachside pottery pieces. You can find Swann on Twitter, Instagram and other platforms at @swannscribe.

Tara Lee is of mixed British-Chinese descent. A postdoctoral researcher at HKU, she currently splits her time, like a migratory bird, between Hong Kong and Oxford. She received her PhD on British Romanticism from the University of Oxford, and has received multiple prizes for her writing, including the Jon Stallworthy Poetry Prize, the Keats-Shelley Essay Prize and the Lord Alfred Douglas Sonnet Prize.

Leung, studying at Musashino Art University (Painting), lives and works between Hong Kong, Japan, and the UK.

Henry Wei Leung is the author of *Goddess of Democracy* and an attorney. He lives in Cambridge, Massachusetts with his wife and son.

Louise Leung Fung Yee (b. Hong Kong, 2000) is an internationally published poet whose works usually cover postcolonialism, cultural politics, and family history. They won the 2nd Prize in the HKBU Century Club Citywide English Poetry Competition 2021. Their works have been published in *Cha: An Asian Literary Journal, Asia Art Archive's Ideas Journal, Canto Cutie, Ricepaper Magazine* and *Voice & Verse Poetry*

Magazine. They wish to give voice to Hong Kong's localism through Kongish literature.

Sannya Li 李瑋琳 is an undergraduate student majoring in Comparative Literature and English Studies at the University of Hong Kong. She is a self-taught poet whose works revolve around Hong Kong culture, Hong Kong identity, the body, and mental health. Her work has featured in *Cha: An Asian Literary Journal.*

Shirley Geok-lin Lim, Professor Emerita at University of California Santa Barbara, former Chair Professor of English at the University of Hong Kong, received the Commonwealth Poetry Prize, two American Book Awards, MELUS and Feminist Press Lifetime Achievement Awards; authored 11 poetry collections (most recently *In Praise of Limes*), a memoir, 3 novels, *The Shirley Lim Collection*, three story collections, and edited over 18 anthologies and journal special issues. Her poems have appeared in *The Hudson Review, Feminist Studies, Virginia Quarterly Review*, and been set to music.

Belle Ling received her PhD in Creative Writing at The University of Queensland, Australia. Her recent poetry manuscript *Rabbit-Light* was highly commended in the 2018 Arts Queensland Thomas Shapcott Poetry Prize. Her other manuscript *Grass Flower Head* was shortlisted for the First Book Poetry Prize 2018 of Puncher and Wattmann. Her poem '63 Temple Street, Mong Kok' was a co-winner in the Peter Porter Poetry Prize 2018 held by *The Australian Book Review*. She is now teaching at The University of Hong Kong.

Emerald Liu is a Sino-Belgian writer who has previously written for *The Millions, Drawing Matter,* and *Far Near*. Her poetry has been featured in *Capsule Stories, Poetry Pacific,* and *The Low Countries*. She was invited to join the writers' residency in Paris by deBuren in the summer of 2022. Currently she is the poetry editor at *Kluger Hans*. Her chapbook *Double Happiness* was published by birdbeakbeast press.

Kayla Sik-chi Lui is a comic artist and art director from Hong Kong who currently resides in London. She self-published her first comic book *Dailongfeng Restaurant* in early 2022, as well as co-published the collective magazine *Heavy Flavours* in 2023. Her works attempt to reinterpret new cultural identities and a general chaos in the world.

Ethan Luk was born and raised in Hong Kong. His work has been recognized by *92Y, The Kennedy Center, One Teen Story, Sine Theta Magazine,* and *The Adroit Journal* among others. He is currently an undergraduate at Princeton University.

London and Greek island based poet **Konstandinos (Dino) Mahoney**, won publication of his collection, *The Great Comet of 1996 Foretells* in the 2021 Live Canon collection competition. His first collection, *Tutti Frutti*, was a winner of the Sentinel Poetry Book Competition 2017. He is also winner of the Poetry Society's 2017 Stanza Competition. He teaches Creative Writing at Hong Kong University (visiting lecturer).

Kika Man 文詠玲 (they/them) is a writer from Belgium and Hong Kong. Kika writes about their mixed heritage, mental health, and travelling, about music and blueness. They grapple daily with the question of where one community starts and the other end, they emphasise tenderness and platonic affections above all. They are one of the founding members of Slam-T (spoken word & slam poetry platform) and a PhD Student in Cultural Studies at the Chinese University of Hong Kong researching zines. Kika is the author of *Let the Mourning Come* (Prolific Pulse LLC, 2022) and they have been published in *Capsule Stories, Anti-Heroin Chic, Bridge* and others. You can find Kika on Twitter and Instagram @kikawinling and further on kikawinling.wordpress.com

Neil Martin is a London-based poet who lived in Hong Kong in the years following the handover. His poems have been published in various UK and Chinese literary magazines, including *The Rialto, The North, The Frogmore Papers* and *The Hong Kong Review*.

David McKirdy grew up in Hong Kong in the 1960s and 70s and came to poetry late in life after completing a degree course in the arts at Hong Kong Open University in 1997. His work has been published in numerous anthologies and he has two books of poetry, *Accidental Occidental* and *Ancestral Worship*. He has represented Hong Kong and has read his work in Cairo, Singapore, Rhode Island, Monterey, Shanghai, Hanoi, Manila and Medellin. He repairs classic cars for a living.

Nadee is originally from Sri Lanka and the mother of two children. She has always been energetic and lively, so she finds no problem in making new friends. She likes swimming, baking, dressmaking, writing, and reading books. She also participates in volunteer work in the community. She loves her family very much and enjoys spending time with them.

Collier Nogues is Assistant Professor of Creative Writing at the Chinese University of Hong Kong. She writes at the intersection of digital and documentary poetics, with an emphasis on making connections across decolonisation and demilitarisation movements in the U.S. and in the Pacific. Her poetry collections include the hybrid print/interactive volume *The Ground I Stand On Is Not My Ground* (2015) and *On the Other Side, Blue* (2011).

Florence Ng was born and lives in Hong Kong. She handmade and self-published her first poetry collection, *Book of Shoes* 鞋子集, and her poems have appeared in various publications including *Su Yeh Literature, Ming Pao* and *Mingled Voices 2.* She has won Youth Literary Awards for her work. Her first bilingual collection *Wild Boar in Victoria Harbour* was published by Kubrick in 2019. In 2021, she created the online poetry journal *Pause for Paws* to celebrate people's love for their pets and animals.

Chioma Onuoha is a writer from Hong Kong. She began writing poetry in 2019. She brings a level of nihilistic amusement to her work. Her inspiration for writing comes from the complications of belonging, understanding what home is and the potential chaos found in quiet moments. She is also the author of 'How to Make a Mixed Baby' (2nd Place in HKBU Citywide Poetry Competition 2020).

Mani Rao is the author of twelve poetry books including *Love Me In A Hurry* (2022), *Sing to Me* (2019), *Ghostmasters* (2010) and *Echolocation* (2003 and 2014); and three books in translation from Sanskrit including *Saundarya Lahari: Wave of Beauty* (HarperCollins 2022), Adi Shankara's paean to the divine feminine. She has a PhD in religious studies and a book of research into mantra — *Living Mantra: Mantra, Deity and Visionary Experience Today* (Cham Springer 2019). Rao has published poems and essays in journals and anthologies including *Wasafiri, POETRY, Fulcrum, WestCoastLine, Bloodaxe Book of Contemporary Indian Poets* and *Penguin Book of the Prose Poem*, performed at festivals including NY PEN World Voices, The Age Melbourne Writers' Festival and Hong Kong International Literary Festival, and held writing residencies at Iowa International Writing Program, Omi Ledig House and IPSI

Canberra. She lived in Hong Kong between 1993 and 2005, where she worked for Star TV heading Marketing and Corporate Communications.

Born in England, **Harry Ricketts** is Emeritus Professor at Te Herenga Waka Victoria University of Wellington, New Zealand. He has published around 30 books, including literary biographies – *The Unforgiving Minute: A Life of Rudyard Kipling* (1999) and *Strange Meetings: The Poets of the Great War* (2010) – personal essays, and twelve collections of poems (most recently *Selected Poems* in 2021). He lived in Hong Kong as a child (1958-1960) and later lectured at the University of Hong Kong (1974-1977).

Kate Rogers' next poetry collection, *The Meaning of Leaving*, is forthcoming with Montreal-based publisher, Ace of Swords (AOS) in early 2024. Her poems recently appeared in *SubTerrain* and *Looking Back at Hong Kong: An Anthology of Writing and Art* (Cart Noodle Press). Kate's reviews have appeared in *The Goose, Ricepaper,* and *Prism International*. Learn more at https://katerogers.ca/. Kate Rogers is a co-director of Art Bar, Toronto's oldest poetry–only reading series.

Xiao Yue Shan is a poet. *How Often I Have Chosen Love* was published in 2019. *Then Telling Be the Antidote* will be published in 2023. www.shellyshan.com.

James Shea is the author of two poetry collections, *The Lost Novel* and *Star in the Eye*, both from Fence Books. He has received grants from the Fulbright U.S. Scholar Program, Hong Kong Arts Development Council, National Endowment for the Arts, and Vermont Arts Council. He is an Associate Professor and the Director of the Creative and Professional Writing Programme at Hong Kong Baptist University.

Huiwen Shi 時惠文 is a bilingual educator, researcher, and writer. Her research interests lie in contemporary poetics, life writing, and service-learning. Her new course, 'Storytelling for Understanding: Refugee Children in Hong Kong', uses personal narratives as an instrument to facilitate cultural learning and community service. She writes theatre reviews in Chinese, and creative nonfiction and poetry in English. She is currently a columnist for *2rulesofwriting*. An ardent lover of literature, Wen believes in the magic of words and their healing power.

Madeleine Slavick 思樂維 is the author of several books of photography, poetry and non-fiction, and an artist with exhibitions across several continents. She has residency rights in Hong Kong, USA, and Aotearoa New Zealand.

Tegan Smyth is a poet with roots in Hong Kong and Australia. She was born in Sydney (Gadigal) and raised between Australia and Hong Kong, with parents hailing from both places. Her work has been published in *Cha: An Asian Literary Journal, Voice & Verse Poetry Magazine, Twin Cities Anthology, KongPoWriMo* and *The Economist.* In addition to her writing, Tegan is the founder of a grassroots refugee charity in Hong Kong called Grassroots Future.

Stella So graduated from the School of Design of the Hong Kong Polytechnic University. Her final year project, *Very Fantastic* (animation), was the winner of the 8th Hong Kong Independent Short Film Competition in 2002 and was invited to a couple of film festivals abroad. Presented in a Chinese copybook, the animation based itself on the city's old districts to induce readers' reverie and expectation to Hong Kong's culture. So's published works include *Very Fantastic, City of Powder — The Disappearing Hong Kong, The Old Girl's Diary* etc.

Chris Song has published four collections of poetry and many volumes of poetry in translation. Song received an 'Extraordinary Mention' at Italy's UNESCO-recognised Nosside World Poetry Prize 2013 and won the Young Artist Award at the 2017 Hong Kong Arts Development Awards. In 2019, he won the 5th Haizi Poetry Award in China. He has been Editor-in-Chief of *Voice & Verse Poetry Magazine* since 2015. He was Executive Director of the International Poetry Nights in Hong Kong from 2014 to 2021 and co-founded the Hong Kong Poetry Festival Foundation in 2018. Song is an assistant professor at the Department of Language Studies (UTSC) with a graduate appointment at the Department of East Asian Studies (UTSG) of the University of Toronto.

Hilary Tam (she/her) is a student and sandwich enthusiast from Hong Kong. She can usually be found taking long walks or listening to Christmas music. Her writing appears in *White Wall Review, Kissing Dynamite, The Lumiere Review* and more.

Eddie Tay is an Associate Professor at the Department of English, Chinese University of Hong Kong. He is the author of four collections of poetry. His recent academic book is *Hong Kong as Creative Practice* (Palgrave, 2023). Originally from Singapore, he has lived in Hong Kong since the early 2000s, thus gaining inspiration for his writing from both cities.

Jennifer Lee Tsai is a poet, editor and critic. She was born in Bebington and grew up in Liverpool. She is a fellow of The Complete Works programme for diversity and innovation and a Ledbury Poetry Critic. She received a Northern Writers Award for Poetry in 2020 and is a winner of the 2022 Women Poets' Prize. Her latest poetry pamphlet *La Mystérique* (2022) is published by Guillemot Press.

Michael Tsang is a poet, a writer, an academic. He swims across languages and cultures, particularly East Asian ones: Cantonese, Mandarin, Japanese, English (and some Korean). He teaches Japanese and Asian cultures at Birkbeck College, University of London. His works have appeared in *Wasafiri, Cha: An Asian Literary Journal, Voice & Verse Poetry Magazine, Eunoia Review*, and others.

Chris Tse is New Zealand's 13th Poet Laureate. He is the author of three collections published by Auckland University Press: *How to be Dead in a Year of Snakes, HE'S SO MASC,* and *Super Model Minority*. He and Emma Barnes co-edited *Out Here: An Anthology of Takatāpui and LGBTQIA+ Writers from Aotearoa*.

Silvia Tse was born and raised in Hong Kong. She currently lives in Durham. She is the co-founder and editor-in-chief of KongPoWriMo (Hong Kong Poetry Writing Month), the local and bilingual alternative to literary initiatives NaPoWriMo, SingPoWriMo and SeaPoWriMo. In between poem-ing and essay-ing, she can be found collecting rocks, painting and climbing, though never at the same time.

Roland Tsoi (they/them), born in Scotland to Chinese parents with roots in Hong Kong, are a poet who effortlessly blend their cultural heritage into their work. They have been published in *The Instant Noodle Literary Review* and *trash to treasure lit*.

Lian-Hee Wee is a phonologist whose libertarian political views are founded on a naïve sense of empirical rationalism that believes rights and responsibilities apply even to predator-prey relationships. Animals also demonstrate how without government they have formed sustainable societies, contrary to doctrines driven by human incarnation of *Animal Farm*'s Squealer. Often frustrated by the ineffability of feelings, Lian-Hee is readily intoxicated by affection and alcohol, although when offered either, he might flee. He makes the guqin and xiao he plays.

Victoria Wilhelmine Walvis used to live in Mong Kok, Kowloon, and then she lived on Lamma, a subtropical island without llamas in Hong Kong. One and a half years ago, she moved to Florence, Italy. She is part England and part Holland, with a passion for moving words small distances on paper, speaking inexpertly in Italian, and wild swimming with a lot of splashing. She is powered by coffee, but it will not sponsor her. Former Peel Street Poet, she has performed for *The Economist* and HK International Literary Festival. She is learning to dance the Lindy Hop.

Wawa is a Hong Kong poet. Her books include *Pei Pei the Monkey King* and *Anna and Anna*. She is currently an M.Div. candidate at Harvard Divinity School where she is pursuing a new sacred poetics of creation myths. lomeiwa.com

Mags Webster is a British-born writer based in Western Australia. A graduate of the City University of Hong Kong's MFA in Creative Writing, Mags lived and worked in Hong Kong from 2011 to 2014. Mags' first poetry book *The Weather of Tongues* won Australia's national Anne Elder Award for best debut collection in 2011. Her next collection, *Nothing to Declare*, was shortlisted for the 2021 Australian Prime Minister's Literary Awards.

Nicolette Wong is a writer, editor and translator from Hong Kong. She is the Editor-in-Chief of *A-minor Magazine*, and Writer in Residence at the Research Centre for Human Values, The Chinese University of Hong Kong.

Nicholas Wong is a visual artist and the author of *Crevasse* (Kaya Press, 2015), the winner of the Lambda Literary Award for Gay Poetry, and *Besiege Me* (Noemi Press, 2021), also a Lammy finalist in 2022. His translation has recently appeared in *Ninth Letter, The Georgia Review, Cincinnati Review, Poetry London,* and *Foglifter*.

Jane Wong is the author of two poetry collections: *How to Not Be Afraid*

of Everything (Alice James, 2021) and *Overpour* (Action Books, 2016). Her debut memoir, *Meet Me Tonight in Atlantic City*, is forthcoming from Tin House in May 2023. She is an Associate Professor at Western Washington University.

Hei Yee Hayley Wu 胡禧怡 is a writer and arts administrator based in Hong Kong. Interested in questions of solidarity, localisms and land rights, selected publications include *Sine Theta Magazine, Liminal Review, Rulerless,* and *DATABLEED*. They are currently working on a collaborative poetry zine titled "poozine", and can be found @ahaybale on twitter.

Jerrold Yam is a Singaporean lawyer based in London. He is the author of three poetry collections: *Intruder* (Ethos Books), *Scattered Vertebrae* (Math Paper Press) and *Chasing Curtained Suns* (Math Paper Press). His poems have appeared in *Ambit, Oxford Poetry, Prairie Schooner, The Straits Times* and *Time Out Magazine*. Say hi on Instagram @yam.biguity.

Marco Yan is a Hong Kong-based poet, whose works have appeared in *Guernica, Epiphany*, and *Making Space*. His collection, *Whoever Told Me Not to Dive Headfirst Dove Headfirst & Knew the Taste* was a finalist in the Gaudy Boy Poetry Prize 2022, as well as the Orison Poetry Prize 2022.

Eric Yip 葉晉瑋 was born and raised in Hong Kong. His poems have appeared in *The Poetry Review, The Adroit Journal, Best New Poets,* and elsewhere. He was the 2021 winner of the National Poetry Competition and is currently an undergraduate studying economics at the University of Cambridge.

Born and raised in Hong Kong, **Josephine Yip** is an amateur writer whose works centre around themes of identity and memory. Passionate about language and bilingualism, she creates and translates poetry and prose in English and Chinese. She is currently an undergraduate student in the United States.

Carmen (Kaman) Yiu is an illustrator and writer from Hong Kong and currently based in London. After graduating from a BA degree in Chinese Language and Literature, she worked as a lifestyle reporter for three years in Hong Kong before studying illustration. With experience working with words and affection on drawing, Carmen's works focus on exploring the relationship between words and illustration.

Born in Sacramento, California, **Ethan Yu** is momentarily staying in New York, reading Hegel and Kierkegaard on the side. He can be found on Twitter @ereignisyu.

Portia Yu is a poet born and raised in Hong Kong. She is fascinated by folklore and mythology, and she enjoys writing poems in which reality turns inside out. Her work has appeared or is forthcoming in several online literary journals including *Worm Moon Archive, celestite poetry* and *Crow & Cross Keys*.

'Lion Rock' by Carmen (Kaman) Yiu

ENDORSEMENTS

'What a thrill to be invited into this raucous city of poems.

As Walt Whitman once said, we must write poems that sing of the body and of the soul.

These are the people's poems: Filling our hearts and minds with empires past and dreamscapes of the present: Cantonese opera wafting through windows, the buzz of taxis and street hawkers, landmark pagodas, magical star ferry rides and endless kettles of chrysanthemum tea, dim sum and noodle shops. The atmosphere is alive with brain-teasing pigeon dialects... sizzling avant-garde experiments and melancholic love songs. Mixing the sacred and the profane, the sublime and the quotidian –for all the light shows and glistening skyscrapers shouting prosperity and future, the people's Hong Kong never leaves the imagination. Those of us who stay, those of us who went away, never lost our feeling of specialness. We are forever proud outsiders: tough yet kind, ironic yet sincere, nostalgic yet futuristic, compassionate yet catastrophic...As Emerald Liu declares: "this city is a maze in which I centre myself." We are Hong Kongers to the core and will defend our cantankerous vivid imagination against all invaders and occupiers. Our poetry is the ultimate expression of freedom and is a harbinger of all that is wondrous and possible!'

Marilyn Chin, Professor Emerita, San Diego State University

'To be a poet is to be 'commensurate with a people,' and *Where Else: An International Hong Kong Poetry Anthology* embraces this Whitmanesque notion. This extraordinary anthology is not just commensurate with the people of the city, it also captures the multitude that is Hong Kong, including all its five senses, history, memory and truths, the hearts and minds of its body politic. Editors Jennifer Wong, Jason Eng Hun Lee and Tim Tim Cheng deserve a 21st Century applause for this 21st Century necessary compilation of 106 poems. Read it, and listen to what these poems have to say. Now.'

Xu Xi (許素細), Jenks Chair in Contemporary Letters, College of the Holy Cross, Worcester, Massachusetts| Co-founder of Authors at Large

'This ambitious, all-encompassing anthology edited by Jennifer Wong, Jason Eng Hun Lee and Tim Tim Cheng is a most timely publication. It comes at a new turning point in both writing in Hong Kong and writing in the Hong Kong Chinese British diaspora; all three editor/poets are representatives of that reinvigorated diasporic writing community. This anthology provides a window onto an exciting and vibrant poetry that is already challenging preconceptions about the Chineseness, Englishness and Hongkongness of a new lyricism in the English language. These are poems born out of two decades of uncertainty and instability, and yet all are either grounded in or haunted by a place that will long remain a source of wonderment: Hong Kong.'

Gregory B. Lee, Professor, School of Chinese Studies, University of St. Andrews | Fellow of the Hong Kong Academy of the Humanities

'I can think of no better way to encapsulate the cosmopolitan diversity of Hong Kong today than through its poetry. *Where Else: An International Hong Kong Poetry Anthology* provides the reader with a host of fascinating and rich insights into the vibrancy of contemporary Anglophone voices, ably anthologised and edited by Jennifer Wong, Jason Eng Hun Lee, and Tim Tim Cheng. The Leeds Centre for New Chinese Writing is delighted to support this publication.'

Frances Weightman, Director of The Leeds Centre for New Chinese Writing

ABOUT VERVE POETRY PRESS

Verve Poetry Press is a quite new and already award-winning press that focused initially on meeting a local need in Birmingham - a need for the vibrant poetry scene here in Brum to find a way to present itself to the poetry world via publication. Co-founded by Stuart Bartholomew and Amerah Saleh, it now publishes poets from all corners of the UK - poets that speak to the city's varied and energetic qualities and will contribute to its many poetic stories.

Added to this is a colourful pamphlet series, many featuring poets who have performed at our sister festival - and a poetry show series which captures the magic of longer poetry performance pieces by festival alumni such as Polarbear, Matt Abbott and Genevieve Carver.

The press has been voted Most Innovative Publisher at the Saboteur Awards, and has won the Publisher's Award for Poetry Pamphlets at the Michael Marks Awards.

Like the festival, we strive to think about poetry in inclusive ways and embrace the multiplicity of approaches towards this glorious art.

www.vervepoetrypress.com
@VervePoetryPres
mail@vervepoetrypress.com